PRESERVING THE TASTE

PRESERVING THE TASTE

Edon Waycott

Hearst Books
New York

I gratefully and lovingly dedicate this book to my mother who showed me the way, and to my father who paid for it.

It is the policy of William Morrow and Company, Inc., and its imprints and affiliates, recognizing the importance of preserving what has been written, to print the books we publish on acid-free paper, and we exert our best efforts to that end.

Library of Congress Cataloging-in-Publication Data

Waycott, Edon.
Preserving the Taste / Edon Waycott.
p.   cm.
Includes index.
ISBN 0-688-10342-1
1. Canning and preserving.   I. Title.
TX601.W39 1993
641.4′2—dc20   92-22669   CIP

Printed in the United States of America

First Edition

1 2 3 4 5 6 7 8 9 10

BOOK DESIGN BY LINDA KOCUR

ACKNOWLEDGMENTS

It was my agent, Maureen Lasher, who sparked the idea for this book. Thanks to her, and to Eric, for lots of assistance and for always returning the jars. Harriet Bell has been a patient, encouraging, constructively critical editor, and a sincere pleasure to work with. My thanks to Nancy Silverton and Mark Peel who first tasted my jam on the first baguettes made at La Brea Bakery. Pairing these preserves with that incomparable bread was an honor. Thanks to the organic farmers who supply me with splendidly flavorful produce: especially Bob Polito for the best Meyer lemons, oranges, grapefruits, and passionfruit; Donna Sherrill for her perfect apples, pomegranate juice, and lots of information; Karl from Abundant Foods; Tutti Frutti Farm; and Pamela Boyar.

And special appreciation to my two wonderful children, Brad and Jennifer, who never failed to give me an honest assessment of a new recipe and kept my kitchen filled with eager tasters; and to my very loyal and loving husband who is the best partner in any project and who has now learned to eat critically.

PRESERVING CHILDREN

Take one large grassy field, one half dozen children, three small dogs, and walk along a narrow strip of brook, pebbly if possible. Mix the children with dogs, and empty them into the field, stirring constantly. Sprinkle the entire with daisies and buttercups, pour brook gently over pebbles, and cover all with a deep blue sky and bake in hot sun for several hours. When children are thoroughly browned they may be removed. They will be found right and ready for setting away to cool in the bathtub.

Mrs. Estes
Buck's County (Pennsylvania) *Cookbook,* 1950

CONTENTS

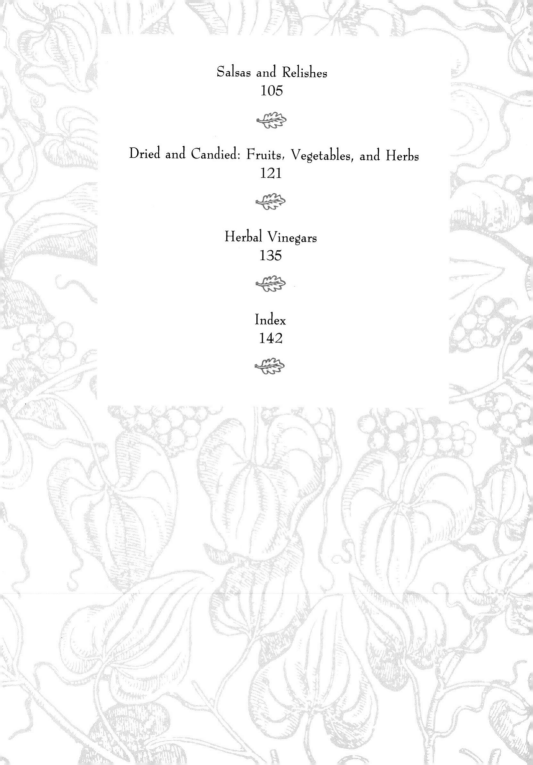

INTRODUCTION

My grandmother in North Carolina had a real old-fashioned farm cellar: dirt floor, cobwebs, damp smell, and floor-to-ceiling jars containing everything from the summer's garden. Whole tomatoes wedged tightly against the glass sides, her own versions of ketchup and tomato juice, corn in every form—creamed, in succotash, on the cob, corn relish—pickles, chow-chow relish, black-eyed peas, spiced grapes, Concord grape jam made from the heavy bunches of enormous purple velvet grapes that hung from the arbor just to the left of the back porch, all labeled, dated, and waiting in the dark for winter. Later I lived in the Northeast and Midwest, and I now make my home in California. Wherever I have gone, I have made jams, jellies, and preserves inspired by those early memories. I would choose fruits and vegetables native to each region: Georgia Belle white peaches, too delicate to be shipped, to make a blush-colored jam; wild blackberries from the mountains of western North Carolina for midnight purple jelly; black-eyed peas for a spicy salsa; tiny new pods of okra for a crunchy pickle; Cape Cod beach plums with their peculiar tartness for jelly; tiny kernels of sweet white corn from local New Jersey truck farms for relish. Now I have juicy red plums, pomegranates, apricots, and figs in my own backyard. My garden is also home to forty varieties of geraniums, twelve of which are the scented leaf kind. Wanting to take advantage of their heady perfume, I made jellies by steeping the leaves in apple juice. Everyone who tasted them was intoxicated by them. Geraniums are easy to grow, yet I've never seen a single jar of jelly for sale.

Home preserving, whether it's an exotic or an indigenous product, gives the cook ultimate control over ingredients, flavors, and cost. In my kitchen I don't need to compromise on quality. I can make jam with less sugar, pickles with less salt, preserved roasted peppers with no additives or artificial colors. My own imagination and the rules of chemistry are the only limits. I can do what commercial manufacturers can't: make small batches so that quality is never sacrificed, constantly look for ways to improve upon common flavors such as strawberry, and create new products.

Since I always like to share whatever I make, I brought a few jars to work with me in 1989. At the time I was managing La Brea Bakery in Los Angeles, owned by Nancy Silverton and Mark Peel, and homemade jam seemed a natural companion to their wonderful country breads. Nancy and Mark were about to open their restaurant, Campanile, and after tasting my jams Nancy asked if I would supply the restaurant's breakfast café. Of course I said yes; the fear came later.

It became obvious that my little hillside garden would be unable to supply enough fruit to meet the demand. I needed to find other sources for fruit. My first stop was the local farmers' market, where I made contact with people who farmed organically. My quest was for the best-tasting fruits; generally I have found that they are pesticide- and chemical-free.

No home kitchen is equipped to cook for restaurants of any size, so my next hurdle was finding commercial kitchen space where I could still produce these products in small batches but do it more often. Because I had only made preserves for friends and family, I was not quite prepared for jumping headlong into boysenberry season with ten flats of berries needing to be cooked and jarred every day. My commitment continued to be focusing on the integrity of these homemade jams without sacrificing any of it for volume. Assured by so many customers that the flavor and consistency of my jams were superior to anything available on the retail level, I shunned all frozen fruit and simply made jam from what was in season. That has meant that during the winter my choices are limited to Apple Cider Butter and Meyer Lemon Marmalade and that by May and June I go a little crazy with plums, mangoes, strawberries, boysenberries, and nectarines.

With each batch I kept altering the sugar, lemon juice, and maceration time, striving for the best combination. I wanted the true flavor of the fruit as well as recognizable chunks of it to be present. For fruits that were low in natural pectin, I added my own pectin made from tart green apples, which allowed more of the flavor of the preserved fruit to emerge. Now I supply several other restaurants with preserves, but I still experiment with unusual fruits and fresh herbs. Sometimes the yield is only one case of a particular flavor, like passion fruit, but it's worth making simply because it isn't on the grocer's shelf.

Since a pure jam made simply with just-picked fruit and a little sugar or pickled *haricots verts* cannot be bought, you should not hesitate to make them at home. Home preserving can mean bringing tastes you never knew existed to the table. Because of better and faster shipping, local farmers engaging in experimental and exotic produce, and the public's curiosity to try something new, such fruits and vegetables as pomegranates, passion fruit, yellow pear tomatoes, baby turnips, golden beets, and miniature squash have become available. Other tantalizing fruits and vegetables never even get mentioned in cookbooks since they have smaller growing zones. Not everything in this book will be accessible to everyone. But with the crisscrossing of regional favorites, something from somewhere else will show up in a roadside stand so you can give it a try.

Preserving at home is a natural outgrowth of America's renewed passion for home favorites, less complicated dishes, and quality, high quality, at any cost. Canning and preserving were tasks our grandmothers had to do; yet I feel that we should look at these not as tiresome chores but as pleasurable responsibilities. In this decade, food issues are focused on the environment (organic farming, recycling), health (less sugar, salt, and fat), and taste (intense, pure, and new). This is a book for today's cook who wants a healthy, superior, unique preserved product made in the home kitchen.

Edon Waycott

PRESERVING INFORMATION

INGREDIENTS

Making preserves is a way of putting on hold those wonderful seasonal tastes from fruits and vegetables so that you can enjoy their pleasures all year round. Granted, there is nothing quite like the taste of freshly harvested produce, but by using exactly this quality for the fruits and vegetables you preserve, that "fresh-from-the-farm" flavor will be in every jar.

A pomegranate tree in the front yard and fig, apricot, avocado, orange, lemon, lime, and tangerine trees in the backyard provide me with enough inspiration and fruit to make jars of jam. But what if you don't have a small orchard of fruit trees? Take heart in knowing that there are plenty of sources for fruits and vegetables. While I love to grow anything, and the more esoteric the better, everything in my garden must have a culinary or utilitarian purpose since space is limited. I grow varieties of vegetables, herbs, and fruits that are either unavailable commercially or are just too expensive. I visit local farmers' markets or wholesale produce companies for the large quantities of fruit I need to make jam for my clients. Sometimes, if I'm lucky, a bumper crop from a neighbor's backyard can provide a windfall. The owners of the tree may have no interest in making use of their fruit, but they would appreciate a jar or two of the jelly made from it. Many people are happy for you to bring a basket and pick whatever you want.

One of my favorite backyard fruits is the Meyer lemon. It is very sweet with a lemon-orange flavor that makes an extraordinary marmalade, but because the tree carries a disease that attacks other citrus, it is not commercially grown. Fortunately, there are trees in residential areas where I live in California that are hardy and bear prolifically.

In a southern California garden, herbs and vegetables and many fruit trees thrive in the warm days and cool nights with very little maintenance. Since I mostly grow things to use in cooking, the herb garden takes up a large amount of space. Poking up through the showier herbs are four kinds of mint. Not satisfied with just the common spearmint, which still has the truest and cleanest flavor, I planted an English mint (which I now pull out by the yard), pineapple mint with a beautiful variegated leaf, and apple mint. Though I grow my mints in the garden, they also will do well in the confines of a pot in partial sun. I also grow two kinds of thyme (silver and lemon), rosemary, lemon verbena, lemon balm, marjoram, Greek oregano, four varieties of lavender, summer and winter savory, and nasturtiums. In the summer I plant the annual herbs: parsley, three varieties of basil, and chervil. When I'm cooking I always need ideas for new seasonings and often the answer is growing just outside the kitchen door.

Besides the herbs, I grow tomatoes, but since the huge beefsteak variety is available at the local farmers' market, I plant the tiny yellow teardrop tomatoes instead. If grown in large plastic pots with wire supports, they can be started indoors and moved outside when the weather begins to warm. Beans, like tomatoes, can be planted in a large pot with verticle supports and moved out on a sunny apartment balcony. *Haricots verts,* ultra-thin French beans, take up very little room. What a treat they are! I have seen these beans in the market for as much as eight dollars a pound.

If you can't grow what you need yourself, the next best thing is to trek out to a farm where you can pick your own. Then there are local farmers' markets and roadside stands where fruits and vegetables have never seen cold storage, are handled far less than what ends up in supermarkets, and are there only in season. Keep in mind that the fruit you want for making jam needs to be ripe, neither soft and mushy nor hard, but not necessarily picture perfect.

If you want to buy produce in quantity and don't live near an agricultural area, ask the manager at a restaurant where you like the vegetables and fruit for the name of his produce supplier. He may be willing to sell to you. Ask for "seconds" or "number twos." Sold by the case, or perhaps a twenty-pound minimum, this grade of fruit is ripe but not quite as perfect looking as "number ones." It is ideal for jams and jellies and far less expensive than what you find in the supermarket.

Always look around at what is grown in your area and make the most of that. Having lived all across the United States, I know there are wonderful indigenous fruits everywhere. Even with all the variety California growers can produce, I can't have the beach plums of Cape Cod, the cherries of Michigan, the tiny huckleberries of the Pacific Northwest. Since the recipes in this book call for much less sugar and salt than usual and use homemade pectin whenever possible, your local or backyard produce will make the best preserves.

EQUIPMENT

Bowls Fruits and some vegetables contain acids that react with aluminum. Stainless steel bowls are a good alternative: lightweight, inexpensive, and nonbreakable. They can also be used to hold lids in boiling water. Glass, ceramic, or heavy plastic containers are also acceptable.

Candy or Jelly Thermometer A thermometer with a metal clamp for attaching to the side of the pan to determine correct jelling temperature.

Cheesecloth Loosely woven cotton, for straining juice from softened fruit and pulp.

Colander A large-hole strainer, for draining washed or salted vegetables and fruits.

Cooling Rack For cooling jars lifted from a hot-water bath. A rack allows air to circulate on all sides of the jar.

Fine Mesh Skimmer Shaped like a long-handled flattened strainer with extremely fine wire mesh, for collecting and removing the foam and scum that accumulate while jelly is boiling.

Food Processor or Food Mill An electric or manual grinder for pureeing fruits or vegetables, either before or after cooking.

Funnel A one-size canning funnel looks like an open-bottom cup shaped to fit both regular and widemouthed canning jars, for keeping the rims of jars clean while filling.

Jars Only the so-called Mason jar should be used for home canning. It is a glass jar with a two-part top. Sizes range from a half-pint to a pint to a quart to half-gallon in narrow and widemouthed widths.

Jar Lifter Similar to tongs but larger, stronger, and coated with soft plastic for removing jars from a hot-water bath.

Jelly Bag A mesh bag suspended by a metal holder to hold cooked or mashed fruit, allowing the juices to drain. The bag should always be dampened first so that it is less likely to absorb liquid from the fruit. Never squeeze the jelly bag in order to extract more juice; any mashing or squeezing will cause a cloudy jelly.

Labels Needed to record the contents and the date made. Decorative labels can be purchased, but it is easy to design your own.

Ladles Like a gravy spoon, with a capacity of at least eight ounces and a spout on one side for pouring hot liquids and jams or jellies more easily into jars.

Paring Knife A knife with a three- or four-inch blade, which is the proper size for removing peels from fruit.

Potato Masher A tool to crush fruits slightly so that their juices are more easily exuded.

Pots and Pans For cooking jams and jellies it is important to use a heavy, nonaluminum shallow pan with at least a six-quart capacity. Because aluminum can react with acid foods producing undesirable tastes or discoloring fruits, it is best to select heavy weight stainless steel, copper, or enamel-lined cast iron. A preserving pan needs to be wider than its height to facilitate evaporation. An ovenproof pan, for cooking fruit butters, needs to go from stove top to oven and can be a large (eleven- or twelve-inch) cast-iron skillet or a shallow braising pan.

Spoons Long-handled metal spoons are a necessity for stirring boiling liquids. Metal is preferable because wood absorbs flavors and colors. Slotted spoons are for lifting fruit out of syrup. A set of measuring spoons is also essential.

Timer Helpful for keeping track of processing time.

Tongs Long and short kitchen tongs for removing home canning lids from hot water and for other purposes. Not to be used for lifting jars from a hot-water bath (see jar lifter).

Water-Bath Canner Any large covered kettle that is deep enough to allow jar tops to be covered with an inch or two of water may be used. Purchased canners come with a divided wire rack basket to keep the jars from touching the sides or bottom of the pot. A round cake rack placed in the bottom of the kettle can be substituted and is necessary to allow the water to circulate under the jars.

Zester Shaped like a small rake with a row of tiny holes instead of prongs for removing long strands of citrus rind without the bitter white pith. By grasping the handle and pulling the curved metal end over the rind of citrus, the flavorful colored part is easily peeled.

FOOD SAFETY AND HANDLING

For anyone preserving vegetables or fruits at home, food safety and handling are of great concern. Basic methods of handling the food and the jars should be followed scrupulously. An understanding of the causes of spoilage will guide you toward a healthy product. The so-called Mason jar with a two-part lid is recommended for long-term storage. Developed by a tinsmith named John Landis Mason in 1858, the glass jar with a rubber ring and metal gasket replaced the earthenware jugs and bottles, which were sealed with corks or wax. Mason's invention came soon after Louis Pasteur discovered that microorganisms cause spoilage. This reliable new canning container offered the home cook a safe method of preserving; it could be used for fruits, vegetables, and meats. Today's Mason jar comes with a two-part lid in sizes from a half-pint to a half-gallon. For whole vegetables and fruits, select widemouthed jars so filling to capacity will be easier. The jar and the metal band are reusable. You can buy new lids separately.

Sterilizing the Jars and Lids Jars must be cleaned and sterilized for preserving and pickling. Wash the jars in hot suds and rinse in scalding water, or put through the sanitizing cycle of a dishwasher. Immediately place on a rimmed baking sheet and put into a preheated 225° F oven at least 20 minutes before filling. The jars also may be kept in a saucepan of barely simmering water but then they need to be dried with a clean towel before using. The jars must be hot when filled with hot liquid to avoid breakage. Separate the lids from the metal rings. Place the lids in a shallow bowl and pour boiling water over them to soften the rubber seal. Allow to soak for 3 minutes before using. Do not boil directly over heat as that could damage the sealing compound.

Filling the Jars Pack vegetables or fruits tightly into the jars and pour hot or boiling (depending on the recipe) liquid or syrup over them to within 1/2 inch of the top of the jar. This allows headspace, which is necessary for the expansion of food when it is processed and to allow a vacuum to form.

Sealing the Jars With a clean, damp towel, wipe the rim of the jar to remove any drips, which would interfere with sealing, and fit with a hot lid. Tightly screw on a metal ring.

Hot-Water Bath Preserved fruits and vegetables generally need to be processed in a hot-water bath, which destroys microorganisms that would cause spoilage. Place the jars on a rack, without touching, in a deep canning kettle with water to cover by one inch. Cover the kettle and boil for the amount of time specified in each recipe. Remove the jars with a plastic-coated jar lifter to a cooling rack and allow to cool completely before storing. During the heat processing, the contents of the jar expands, forcing some of the air out. The remaining air inside contracts as it cools to create a partial vacuum, which pulls the lids tight against the jar rims. The vacuum and the lid's sealing compound maintain the seal. A popping noise after the contents have cooled is an indication that the seal is complete. To test, press the center of the cooled lid. If it stays depressed, the jar is sealed. If not, refrigerate and eat the contents within two to three weeks or reseal with a new flat lid and repeat the hot-water bath.

Labeling and Storing To avoid confusion, write the name of the product and the date it was canned on a label that will adhere to the jar after it has cooled. Canned foods stored in a cool (below seventy degrees), dark, dry place will retain their flavor, color, and nutritional value for about a year. Warm storage temperatures and light hasten discoloration and flavor changes.

Spoilage A concern of every home preserver is the possibility of spoilage. Since the greatest risk comes in low-acid foods, I have made sure that the recipes in this book contain an acidic solution when the vegetable does not have a high acid content of its own. Suspended in vinegar, or high proportions of vinegar, the preserved foods can then be heated in a hot-water bath to bring the internal temperature to 212°, which kills harmful molds, yeasts, and bacteria. Fruit-based products do not present quite the concern of low-acid vegetables and meats since fruits are naturally acidic and sugar is a natural preservative. When canning low-acid vegetables and meats it is imperative to process in a pressure canner, which can bring the internal temperature up to a safe level. None of the recipes in this book requires this method.

If mold is present when a jar is opened or if the contents smell fermented, the preserves are no longer good and should be discarded. Never determine the safety of home-packed foods by tasting. Judge instead by appearance: a bulging lid, leakage from around the lid, upward-moving bubbles, patches of mold, or foamy or murky appearance. A pleasant odor characteristic of the food canned is a good sign of properly preserved food. Use your eyes, nose, and good sense to detect spoilage. If a food doesn't look or smell right, don't eat it.

PECTIN

Pectin, a naturally occurring substance in fruits and vegetables, is valued for its thickening properties. Pectin content varies not only from fruit to fruit but also from variety to variety. Tart or sour fruits tend to have a higher pectin content. To help you determine if the fruit you are using requires the addition of a homemade pectin stock, here is a list of fruits high and low in natural pectin. Combining a fruit high in pectin with one low in pectin is another way of raising the pectin content of a jam up to a jelling level.

To test for pectin, put one tablespoon of fruit juice into a bowl with three tablespoons of rubbing alcohol. Swirl the mixture around for a minute until clotting develops. A large clot indicates a high pectin level; a few small clots indicate a medium level; and scattered small beads indicate a low level. *Do not taste this mixture!*

Fruits high in pectin:

    Tart apples, such as pippins, Granny Smiths, crab apples

    Citrus fruits: lemons, limes, oranges, grapefruits, tangerines

    Cranberries

    Currants

    Gooseberries

    Guavas

    Sour plums

    Quinces

Fruits medium in pectin:

    Sweet apples, such as Golden Delicious, Red Delicious, MacIntosh, Rome

    Blackberries

    Boysenberries

    Cherries, such as Queen Anne, Ranier, Bing

    Elderberries

    Loganberries

    Melons

    Olallieberries

Fruits low in pectin:

    Apricots

    Blueberries

    Figs

    Grapes

    Nectarines

    Peaches

Pears

Pineapples

Plums, such as Santa Rosa, Black, Greengage, Damson

Raspberries

Rhubarb

Strawberries

HOMEMADE PECTIN

Tart, slightly underripe green apples are the best choice for making your own pectin. They have a very high concentration of pectin, are easily available and inexpensive, and don't carry a strong flavor of their own. With homemade pectin, you need to add no more sugar than necessary to bring the fruit to the point of sweetness, unlike commercial pectin products, which rely on a formula of more sugar than fruit to jell. Adding homemade pectin stock to fruits that are lacking in natural pectin will not interfere with the flavor of the original fruit; it will help bring the fruit mixture to a soft-set without excessive cooking.

I have included recipes, however, that call for a commercial pectin. *A liquid commercial pectin is not interchangeable with homemade pectin.* I prefer to use commercial pectin for savory jellies like the herbal jellies and Five Pepper Jelly, or when there simply isn't enough fruit base to jell the mixture.

Making pectin at home is a simple process, much like making jelly. I have not given an amount of apples. I personally would cook up to fifteen pounds at a time to make about two quarts, which can be frozen in one-cup, two-cup, or even smaller portions. Then when summer fruits are available, my time—and yours—can be spent making jam.

Underripe Granny Smiths, pippins, green apples, washed and cut into eighths (do not core or peel)

2 cups water for each pound of apples

1. Place the apples and water in a large stockpot or soup kettle, cover, and bring to a boil. Reduce heat and simmer 20 minutes or until apples are tender. Remove from heat and allow to cool slightly.

2. Pour the pulp and juice through a jelly bag or line a large bowl with dampened cheesecloth, pour the pulp and juice through, gather the corners of the cheesecloth, and tie in a knot. Suspend from a cabinet knob or handle and allow to drip into a bowl overnight.

3. The next day, measure the apple juice and pour into a large pot. Bring to a boil over high heat and cook until reduced by half. Refrigerate and use within 4 days or pour into containers and freeze for up to 6 months.

An easy way to determine reduction is to measure the depth of the liquid in the pan with a plastic ruler before boiling. Re-measure as liquid reduces. No need to pour into measuring cup!

JAMS, JELLIES, MARMALADES, AND PRESERVED FRUITS

apturing the flavor and color of ripe fruit is my goal when making jam. If you choose tree-ripened fruit at the peak of the season, preferably locally grown, producing a great-tasting jam is already simplified. Four things to watch out for in making jam are: overcooking, adding too much pectin, oversweetening, and home canning safety. Since the only components of jam and jelly are fruit, acid, pectin, and a sweetener, every one must be high quality and perfectly balanced with the others. If you let nature and the raw ingredients work for you, you should be able to close your eyes and tell exactly what kind of jam you are eating. And that taste should make you say "Wow!" Slightly underripe fruit contains more pectin and can be mixed with perfectly ripe fruit to ensure better jelling properties. Because I prefer a softer jam than the commercial kind, I usually use homemade pectin (page 13) to slightly thicken fruits that have little or no pectin of their own. Acid, usually lemon juice, activates the pectin to jell the fruit. It also gives ripe fruit a little spark. The sweetener helps extract the natural juices and then, in cooking, thickens them. Sugar also serves as a natural preservative in jams and jellies when safe rules of canning are followed.

Many of the jams and preserves in this book can be used to fill tarts, top cheesecake, spread on pancakes, fill crêpes, stir into yogurt, or bake in a muffin for a surprise bite. These preserves are simple, pure, and loaded with fruit flavor; they enhance whatever they are spooned on.

Fruit preserves and jellies should be cooked in pans that will not react to their acid content. These include heavy stainless steel, anodized aluminum, enamel-coated cast iron, or lined copper. All should be shallower than their width and of heavy weight. A braising pan, a six-quart Dutch oven, even a large straight-sided sauté pan can be used. Choose a pan with a capacity of nearly double the volume of the recipe so there will be less chance of boiling over. Cooking times in these recipes are based on pans that are no more than six inches in depth. A stockpot is necessary when merely cooking fruit to a soft stage but not to make the preserves.

When the fruit mixture comes to a boil, lower the heat to allow even simmering, with bubbles still breaking the surface. Stir often to avoid any sticking to the bottom of the pan. A foam will often accumulate on top and should be skimmed off. It is a result of the air combining with the fruit cells and sugar, and, although harmless, may cloud a jelly or be visible in a jar of jam. After the allotted time for cooking has elapsed, turn off the heat and proceed with the wrinkle test on page 18. Keep in mind that all jams and jellies continue to set during cooling, and it is my preference to have a jam soft-set rather than too firm. This is one of the characteristic differences between commercial preserves and homemade ones. But if your test is too liquid, continue to cook at a simmer and recheck at five-minute intervals.

When the jam is ready, keep the heat on low while filling the jars. Jars should be hot and sterilized, lids should be immersed in boiling water for at least three minutes prior to using, and a canning funnel and clean, damp towel should be accessible. Using a ladle, pour the hot liquid through the funnel into the jar and fill to within a half inch of the top. If any drips occur, wipe the rims clean with the towel and place a new lid on top of the jar. Screw on a metal band to hold the lid in place as the contents cool.

Jellies that fail to jell could be the result of too little sugar, pectin or acid, or cooking. You can use these flavorful syrups as toppings for ice cream or pancakes or as the base for milk shakes. But to remedy the situation of too soft jelly, recook the jelly with the aid of a little powdered pectin.

Measure the jelly to be cooked, and for each quart stir together ¼ cup water, 4 teaspoons powdered pectin, and ¼ cup sugar. Bring this mixture to a boil, stirring constantly, in a deep pot. Add the soft jelly and bring again to a full boil for 30 seconds. Turn off the heat, skim off any foam from the top, pour into hot, sterilized jars, and seal. Check seals after 24 hours. The middle of the lid should be slightly concave, unable to be pressed down. If it did not seal, store the jar in the refrigerator and consume within a few weeks. Or remove the metal band and lid, reheat the contents of the jar, and pour into a clean, hot sterilized jar and seal with a new lid and metal band. The lid can only be used once. The metal bands may be washed and reused.

If a recipe calls for a hot-water bath, place the jars in a kettle deep enough for them to be covered with at least 1 inch of water. Bring the water to a boil, cover the kettle, and process for length of time specified in the recipe. For details, see page 8.

Essential to success in making jam and jelly are your own good taste and good sense. Use these recipes as a base but be flexible and spontaneous. Every batch of fruit varies in ripeness, water content, and sweetness, so it is always important to taste your product. Cool a spoonful of jam on a saucer halfway through the cooking time and taste it, keeping in mind that everything will become more concentrated by the end because of evaporation. Season the batch with sugar or lemon juice at this time. It's also okay to add another half cup of sugar or a couple teaspoons of lemon juice at the very end of cooking a pot of jam or preserves.

Jellies are a little trickier in their proportions and are not quite as forgiving. Cook only the amounts listed in these recipes at any given time. They cannot be doubled or tripled with the same results.

Wrinkle Test The wrinkle test is a method of testing the readiness of jam or jelly. When the prescribed time for cooking is completed, turn off heat, remove a tablespoon of the jam or jelly to a saucer and place in the freezer for five minutes. Remove saucer from freezer and very slowly draw your finger through the center of the jam. If the surface of the mixture wrinkles like the gathers of a skirt, then it is ready to be jarred. Reheat the jam in the pan to the boiling point before ladling.

All jams and jellies need to be sealed in sterilized jars with two-part sealing lids unless you plan to keep them in the refrigerator. I save jars with twist-on lids to fill with jam left over from batches that don't quite come out even. These I store in the refrigerator for my own family's use; they keep for about a month.

Paraffin People used to preserve jams and jellies with a thin layer of melted paraffin (household wax), but this method is no longer recommended.

Jam has a shelf life of about a year if properly sealed. After that time, although it may still be safe to eat, the nutritional value and quality deteriorate. Colors darken even if the jars have been stored away from light. So plan on using or giving away your preserves within the year. You can replenish your supply with the next season's harvest.

APRICOT AND HONEY JAM

I never ate a fresh apricot until I moved to California. I remember without fondness the canned variety or the occasional pieces in fruit cocktail I ate as a child. A jar of apricot preserves was on hand to be melted over a fruit tart, but the contents bore no relation to the fruit for which it was named. So biting into a real-life fresh apricot was like crossing a kind of taste frontier. On our backyard hillside we are fortunate to have a beautiful apricot tree, which is prolific every other year in late June and early July. It's feast or famine, and I greatly miss the apricot feast when we're in the famine year.

Apricots are a neat fruit, one of the easiest to prepare: no peeling necessary, a freestone pit, and firm flesh that makes perfect slices. This sunshine-orange fruit makes a naturally thick and luscious jam that tastes as good on an unbuttered piece of whole wheat toast as on a warm, buttery croissant.

Makes 9 half-pint jars

6 pounds ripe apricots
  (about 50)
2 cups sugar
1/2 cup mild honey, such as
  orange blossom or clover
3 tablespoons lemon juice

1. Wash the apricots. Cut them in half through the natural indentation and remove the pits. Slice each half into 4 lengthwise strips. There should be approximately 4 quarts.

2. Gently combine the apricot slices, sugar, honey, and lemon juice in a large nonreactive bowl. Allow to stand at room temperature for 3 to 4 hours, stirring several times to keep the fruit coated and to help the juices dissolve the sugar.

3. Pour the fruit mixture into a large 6-quart nonreactive shallow preserving pan and bring to a boil over high heat. With a metal spoon or fine mesh skimmer, skim off any foam that forms on top. Reduce heat to medium. Continue cooking, stirring occasionally, for 20 to 30 minutes until the mixture is thick with a few chunks left and appears slightly glazed.

4. Turn off the heat and skim any additional foam. Ladle into hot sterilized jars, wipe rims clean with a damp towel, and seal with new lids and metal rings. Process in a hot-water bath (page 8) for 5 minutes. Remove, cool, check seals, label, and store.

BOYSENBERRY JAM

Boysenberries are a delicious cross between a raspberry and a black-berry, often half as large as your thumb. They are soft and delicate like the raspberry with the distinct tartness and seeds of the black-berry. They begin to appear in farmers' markets in June. Finding a farm that will allow you to pick your own will ensure that this perishable fruit will retain its perfume and firmness in an intensely colored and flavored jam. If the seeds bother you, press about half of the finished mixture through a mesh sieve in small batches, scraping the bottom of the sieve often to collect the thick puree. If a windfall of berries catches you without any homemade pectin in the freezer, reduce two cups of apple cider to one cup and add that to the berries and sugar. It won't be quite as silky and thick, but it will help thicken the jam without having to overcook it. Because this jam is not stiff, it is nice to pour over vanilla ice cream or to nap a plate of freshly made profiteroles, as my friend Liv Blumer does.

Makes 5 half-pint jars

8 cups boysenberries, rinsed and
   lightly packed
3 cups sugar
3 tablespoons lemon juice
1 1/3 cups Homemade Pectin
   (page 13)

1. Combine the berries, sugar, and lemon juice in a large, nonreactive bowl. With a potato masher or large metal spoon, press on the berries to bruise and mash them. Do not puree. Allow to macerate for at least 4 hours at room temperature or refrigerated overnight.

2. Pour the contents of the bowl into a large 6-quart nonreactive shallow preserving pan and place over medium heat. Bring to a boil and stir in the pectin. Continue cooking for 25 to 35 minutes, stirring constantly the last 10 minutes to prevent the bottom from burning. When bubbles begin to change from larger ones here and there to very small ones all over, the jam is ready.

3. Turn off the heat. Ladle the jam into hot sterilized jars, wipe rims clean with a damp towel, and seal with new lids and metal rings. Process in a hot-water bath (page 8) for 5 minutes. Remove, cool, check seals, label, and store.

FIG JAM WITH CANDIED LEMON ZEST

Figs pose a dilemma in our household. We love to eat them right off the tree, often running down the hill to pluck a handful for breakfast, but we also love them preserved with translucent candied lemon zest in a thick, syrupy marmalade. It goes well with whole grain bread or bran muffins, but I like it best on brioche, like a sophisticated Fig Newton.

Makes 5 half-pint jars

4 lemons

3 cups sugar

3 pounds figs, Black Mission,
  White, or Brown Turkey
  (about 60)

1/4 cup fresh lemon juice

1/8 teaspoon ground allspice

1. Remove the zest from the lemons with a zester. Or remove with a paring knife or vegetable peeler and cut into 1/4-inch strips. Cut in half if strips are longer than 1 1/2 inches. There should be about 1 cup of lemon zest. Reserve lemons to use for juice. Bring 1 cup of the sugar and 1 cup water to a boil. Drop in the zest and boil on medium heat until the pieces are translucent and candied. This will take approximately 30 minutes. Remove from the heat, cover the pan, and set aside overnight.

2. The next day, bring a large pot of water to a boil and drop in the figs. Cook for 5 minutes. Drain. When cool enough to handle, cut off the stems. Pulse half of the figs in a food processor until coarsely chopped. Do not puree. There should still be large chunks of fig peel visible. Pour into a large 6-quart nonreactive shallow preserving pan. Cut the remaining figs into eighths and add to the pan.

3. Add ¼ cup water and cook on medium heat for 20 minutes just until water has evaporated and fig peel is tender. Lower the heat, add the remaining 2 cups of sugar, the lemon juice, allspice, and ½ cup of the candied lemon zest without the syrup. Reserve remaining zest for another use. Continue cooking, stirring occasionally, until mixture is slowly bubbling over the entire surface, about 20 to 30 minutes.

4. Ladle the jam into hot sterilized jars, wipe rims clean with a damp towel, and seal with new lids and metal rings. Process in a hot-water bath (page 8) for 5 minutes. Remove, cool, check seals, label, and store.

MANGO JAM

Mangoes are wonderful; their exotic tropical taste immediately awakens your senses. When I acquired an Italian ice-cream machine, mango sorbet was one of my most successful ventures. Because the water content is relatively low and the flesh is dense, the mango loses little of its purity and intensity when frozen. I wasn't sure if the same would be true after the fruit was cooked, but I am happy I tried. The most difficult part about making this jam is finding ripe mangoes. Peak season is summer. You have to choose a mango by feel and aroma, since the color can vary from green to yellow to blush red. A fully ripe mango is as tender as a ripe avocado, and it should smell like a mango. Dense, white, buttery, thick-sliced toast is its best vehicle (except, of course, for a spoon).

Makes 6 half-pint jars

*8 ripe mangoes (about
    ¾ pound each)*
2 cups sugar
*3 tablespoons fresh lime or
    lemon juice*

1. Carefully peel the mangoes. The skin is very bitter so avoid leaving even the smallest trace. Make lengthwise cuts about ½ inch apart through the flesh to the pit. Make crosswise cuts also about

½ inch apart. Slide the knife between the pit and the fruit, separating it into cubes. Don't worry about the shape of the pieces; this jam turns to mush very quickly. There should be about 4 cups of pulp.

2. Mix the pulp with 1½ cups of the sugar and the lime or lemon juice and taste. If it's sweet enough for you, don't add any more sugar. Let stand at room temperature for 3 to 4 hours, stirring occasionally.

3. Pour the mixture into a large heavy pot and slowly bring to a boil. Lower heat and cook for 20 minutes, skim off any foam.

4. Ladle the jam into hot sterilized jars, wipe the rims clean with a damp towel, and seal with new lids and metal rings. Process in a hot-water bath (page 8) for 5 minutes. Remove, cool, check seals, label, and store.

NECTARINE JAM

One of the advantages of making jam from nectarines is that they don't have to be peeled. Leaving the peel on also colors the syrup of the jam ever so slightly rosy.

Makes 6 half-pint jars

8 pounds nectarines, unpeeled
  and sliced into ¹/₂-inch pieces,
  (about 12 cups)
1 cup sugar
1 cup honey
2 tablespoons fresh lemon juice

1. Toss together the sliced fruit and sugar in a large bowl and let stand at room temperature for 3 hours or cover and refrigerate overnight.

2. Place a large colander in a 12-inch skillet and pour the fruit and juice through. Allow to drain for 1 hour. Remove the colander with the fruit to a bowl to collect any additional juices and bring the syrup in the skillet to a boil over high heat. Cook until reduced by half and very syrupy, about 7 minutes.

3. Add the fruit and any accumulated juices and cook, stirring, for 10 minutes. The fruit will soften and the skin will come off and tint the syrup. Process half of the contents of the skillet in a food processor until smooth. This puree will thicken the jam so that the fruit does not need to be cooked further. Return it to the skillet. Add the honey and lemon juice, stir to combine, and taste for additional lemon juice.

4. Bring the mixture back to a simmer and ladle into hot sterilized jars, wipe the rims clean with a damp towel, and seal with new lids and metal rings. Process in a hot-water bath (page 8) for 5 minutes. Remove, cool, check seals, label, and store.

PEAR AND GINGER JAM

Subtly flavored and soft-textured pears come in many varieties during fall and winter. One of the first to appear is the aromatic yellow Bartlett. This is often the least expensive, most abundant, and fastest to ripen. Bosc, D'Anjou, and Comice will most likely be in the produce section too. Mix several different varieties of pear if you like. Also mix ripe and underripe fruit so that some natural pectin is present. Besides, this jam needs long, slow cooking, which would turn very ripe pears into mush. The desired texture is more like a chunky applesauce. I prefer not to put the fruit mixture through a food processor, in order to maintain more of the fruit's true characteristics. This jam pairs best with scones, tea breads, cranberry muffins, or white toast. Slightly warmed, it is perfect with squares of freshly made gingerbread.

Makes 5 half-pint jars

5 pounds small pears, peeled, cored, and cut into 1/4-inch slices (about 20)

2 cups sugar

2 tablespoons minced candied gingerroot, rinsed

2 teaspoons grated lemon zest

1/4 cup fresh lemon juice

1 vanilla bean, split and scraped

1. Toss the pears with the sugar, gingerroot, zest, lemon juice, and vanilla bean in a large bowl. Let stand 3 hours at room temperature or refrigerate overnight.

2. Pour the pear mixture into a large 6-quart nonreactive shallow preserving pan and place over high heat. Bring to a boil, reduce heat to low, and continue cooking for 1½ hours. Stir occasionally. Pieces of pear will still be visible and jam will have thickened to a chunky applesauce consistency. Remove vanilla bean.

3. Ladle the jam into hot sterilized jars and seal with new lids and metal rings. Wipe rims clean with a damp towel. Process in a hot-water bath (page 8) for 5 minutes. Remove, cool, check seals, label, and store.

RASPBERRY JAM

I prefer raspberry jam softer than what you can buy, with a few chunks of berry in the puree. Because raspberries have little natural pectin, I add homemade pectin to shorten the cooking time. The jam would thicken eventually without pectin, but the color would be darker and the berries a puree. Raspberries are sold in *half-pint* baskets, so measure carefully.

Makes 10 half-pint jars

6 pints raspberries (12 cups)
3 cups sugar
1 1/3 cups Homemade Pectin
    (page 13)
2 tablespoons fresh lemon juice

1. Pick over the raspberries for any leaves or unusable fruit. There should be 3 packed quarts. Combine with the sugar in a large bowl and let stand at room temperature for 6 hours or overnight in the refrigerator. Stir occasionally.

2. Stir together the raspberry mixture, pectin, and lemon juice in a large shallow nonreactive preserving pan and place over high heat. Bring to a full boil, skim off foam, then lower heat to medium. Stir often so the bottom does not burn. When the jam is sufficiently thickened, the bubbles on top will become smaller and the jam will

look like bubbling tar. This takes approximately 20 minutes, depending on the size of the pan. If the jam is still too liquid, continue cooking for 5 minutes more and test again.

3. Turn off the heat and remove a tablespoon of jam to a small plate to test. Chill in the freezer for 5 minutes. If the jam is the consistency desired, turn the heat to low while ladling the jam into hot sterilized jars. Wipe rims clean with a damp towel. Seal with new lids and metal rings. Process in a hot-water bath (page 8) for 5 minutes. Remove, cool, check seals, label, and store.

RED PLUM JAM

At the height of the season, I can find at least nine different varieties of plums in my supermarket. For jam, I prefer either the red-skinned Santa Rosa or red-fleshed black plums; both of them turn a beautiful garnet color when cooked. Use organic plums, if possible, since the recipe calls for unpeeled fruit, which shortens the prep time, increases the fiber content, and enhances the color. Plums vary greatly in sweetness; always taste one first to determine the amount of sugar needed and start with the minimum, adding more at the end if needed. The extra sugar will make the jam a bit softer, but chilling will firm it.

Makes 10 half-pint jars

7 pounds ripe but firm Santa
Rosa or black plums or
another variety with either
red skin or red pulp, unpeeled
and quartered (12 cups)
3 cups sugar
2 tablespoons fresh lemon juice

1. Place the plums in a large bowl and stir in the sugar. Let stand at room temperature 4 hours or refrigerate, covered, overnight.

2. Pour the mixture into a large nonreactive shallow preserving pan, add the lemon juice, and cook over medium heat, stirring often, for approximately 30 minutes.

3. Remove a tablespoonful of jam to a chilled saucer and place in the freezer for 5 minutes. If the jam holds together and is the thickness of pudding, taste for sweetness. Additional sugar, if needed, should be added ½ cup at a time and stirred into the jam while it is very hot. Taste after each addition. If the jam is still too liquid, continue cooking for 5 minutes and test again.

4. Reheat the jam and ladle into hot sterilized jars, wipe rims clean with a damp towel, and seal with new lids and metal rings. Process in a hot-water bath (page 8) for 5 minutes. Remove, cool, check seals, label, and store.

TOMATO JAM

Aren't jams fruit based? Yes, and yes, the tomato is a fruit. What may help is some associations like tomato jam on a toasted onion bagel, on a hot corn muffin, on rye bread with cheddar cheese, on a cold meat-loaf sandwich. I'm talking about a savory spread with the consistency of thick jam. (I don't seed the tomatoes, but if you want, you can squeeze the halved tomatoes lightly to seed them before pureeing.)

Makes 4 half-pint jars

8 pounds ripe tomatoes, peeled, cored, and halved

2 teaspoons salt

2 tablespoons sugar

4 tablespoons raspberry vinegar

1/2 teaspoon ground white pepper

4 tablespoons dark brown sugar

1 teaspoon ground cinnamon

1. Puree the tomatoes in batches in a food processor. There should be about 3 quarts. Pour the tomato puree into a large shallow preserving pan and place over medium heat. Stir in the salt and sugar. Bring to a full boil and continue to cook, uncovered, for 30 minutes. At first the mixture will be foamy, but as it begins to reduce, it will thicken and start to stick to the bottom of the pan. At that point add the vinegar, pepper, brown sugar, and cinnamon, and

continue cooking until the jam is very thick and holds its shape when mounded onto a large metal spoon, about 30 minutes more.

2. Ladle the jam into hot sterilized jars and seal with new lids and metal rings. Wipe rims clean with a damp towel. Process in a hot-water bath (page 8) for 5 minutes. Remove, cool, check seals, label, and store. Allow to age for at least 2 weeks before using.

BLACKBERRY JELLY

Of all the fruits, only heavily seeded berries, like blackberries, boy-senberries, or olallieberries, really need to be made into jelly. Making jelly is laborious, messy, and somewhat wasteful. But the final product is intense in flavor and smooth in texture. With homemade pectin, the jelly isn't as sweet or rubbery as commercial jellies.

Makes 4 half-pint jars

*12 cups blackberries or
   boysenberries*
4 cups sugar
1 tablespoon fresh lemon juice
*2 cups Homemade Pectin
   (page 13)*

1. Wash the berries and put them in a large 6-quart pan with ½ cup of water. Crush slightly with the back of a large metal spoon or a potato masher. Cook over medium heat until softened and very juicy, about 10 minutes.

2. Use a jelly bag or line a large bowl with a double layer of dampened cheesecloth that hangs over the rim by 6 inches. Pour in the berry mixture. Gather the corners of the cheesecloth together and tie in a knot. Tie with strong kitchen twine and suspend from cabinet knob over the bowl. There should be 4 cups of juice. The juice can be frozen for up to 3 months or refrigerated for 2 days.

3. When ready to make jelly, pour the juice into a nonreactive deep pot, such as a stockpot. Add the sugar, lemon juice, and pectin. The pot should be deep because when the mixture boils, it swells and foams up to more than five times its original volume. Bring to a boil and continue boiling on high for about 20 minutes, skimming off the foam. Turn off the heat and test by placing a small amount on a saucer and chilling it in the freezer for several minutes. If the jelly passes the wrinkle test (page 18), then it is ready. If not, continue cooking and test again after 5 minutes. This jelly will continue to set after it is jarred.

4. Pour into hot sterilized jars, wipe the rims clean with a damp towel, and seal with new lids and metal rings. Process in a hot-water bath (page 8) for 5 minutes. Remove, cool, check seals, label, and store.

FEIJOA (GUAVA) JELLY

The feijoa, also known as pineapple guava, makes a most exotic jelly. The flesh of this fruit is grainy, somewhat like a pear, but it is perfumed and tart. Though cream to tan in color, the flesh cooks into a beautiful pink jelly. I like it soft. Feijoa jelly is so other-worldly, the soft texture adds to its appeal. In California the feijoa season is a short four to five weeks in November and December. The fruit is imported from New Zealand in spring and early summer but is quite expensive. If you live in the right part of the country, ask a neighbor to share the bounty of a backyard tree in exchange for a couple jars of jelly.

Makes 5 half-pint jars

5 pounds ripe but firm feijoas,
*   unpeeled and quartered*
4 cups sugar
4 teaspoons fresh lemon juice

1. Place the feijoas in a large deep pot. Add water until just beneath the top layer of fruit. Bring to a boil, reduce the heat, and continue to simmer, uncovered, until soft, about 30 minutes. Mash slightly with the back of a spoon.

2. Use a jelly bag or line a large bowl with 2 layers of dampened cheesecloth, allowing about 6 inches to hang over the rim. Carefully pour fruit and liquid into the cheesecloth. Grasp the overhanging

edges and pull together. Tie opposite corners together and suspend from a cupboard knob over the bowl. Allow to drip at least 4 hours or even overnight. Do not squeeze the bag or particles of pulp will come through the cheesecloth and make the jelly cloudy.

3. Measure out 6 cups of juice. If you have more, freeze it until you are able to cook more fruit. Do not cook more than 6 cups at a time. Pour into a large nonreactive shallow preserving pan. Stir in the sugar and lemon juice. Bring to a boil and cook over moderately high heat for 30 minutes. Skim off foam with a fine meshed skimmer or carefully with a metal spoon. Test for jelling as described on page 18. Continue boiling until the proper consistency is reached. When the liquid begins to turn pale pink, it is getting close. The jelly intensifies in color as it stands, so watch carefully when it starts to change.

4. Quickly pour into hot sterilized jars, wipe the rims clean with a damp towel, and seal with new lids and metal rings. Process in a hot-water bath (page 8) for 5 minutes. Remove, cool, check seals, label, and store.

FIVE PEPPER JELLY

This jelly seems very much at home on a piece of warm cornbread, a savory herb biscuit, or a crusty slice of country white. It also gives a quesadilla an interesting, zesty bite when spread on the inside of the flour tortillas before grilling.

Makes 7 half-pint jars

2 large red bell peppers
 (³/4 pound)
1 large green bell pepper
¹/2 small onion, finely chopped
4 jalapeño or serrano chilies,
 seeds and veins removed,
 finely chopped
2 teaspoons salt
5 cups sugar

1¹/2 cups red wine vinegar
¹/2 cup fresh lemon juice
¹/2 teaspoon chili powder
¹/4 teaspoon cayenne
¹/2 teaspoon crushed red pepper
6 ounces commercial liquid
 pectin
2¹/2 teaspoons whole cumin seed,
 toasted

1. Remove the seeds and stems from the bell peppers and cut into 2-inch pieces. Place in a food processor and process until finely chopped. Remove to a colander and combine with the onion, chopped jalapeños, and 1 teaspoon of the salt. Allow to drain for 3 hours. Press to extract as much moisture as possible.

2. Transfer the mixture to a large heavy nonreactive saucepan. Stir in the sugar, vinegar, lemon juice, chili powder, cayenne, crushed red

pepper, and the remaining salt. Bring to a boil, stirring, and cook for 10 minutes. Add the pectin and boil for exactly 1 minute, stirring constantly. Turn off heat, stir in the cumin seed, and allow to stand for 5 minutes.

3. Stir to distribute the chopped peppers evenly and pour into hot sterilized jars. Wipe the rims clean with a damp towel and seal with new lids and metal rings. Process in a hot-water bath (page 8) for 5 minutes. Remove, cool, check seals, label, and store.

LEMON-GINGER-HONEY JELLY

Made with no sugar and no fruit pulp, this jelly relies on honey tempered dramatically with lots of citrus juice and ginger for its flavor. You can use homemade or storebought crystallized ginger-root. It takes little time to make since commercial liquid pectin is used. The jelly is good on whole wheat toast and as a glaze applied to chicken during the last minutes of roasting or barbecuing.

Makes 4 half-pint jars

2 1/4 cups mild honey, such as clover or orange blossom

3/4 cup fresh lemon juice

3/4 cup fresh orange juice

1 tablespoon finely chopped lemon zest (3 lemons)

1 tablespoon finely chopped orange zest (3 oranges)

3 tablespoons minced Crystallized Gingerroot (page 129), rinsed to remove the sugar

3 ounces commercial liquid pectin

1. Bring the honey, lemon juice, orange juice, and lemon and orange zest to a boil in an 8-quart nonreactive saucepan. Stir in the ginger. When mixture comes back to a boil, add the pectin and return to a boil. Boil on high heat for exactly 1 minute, stirring constantly. Remove from the heat and stir for 3 minutes to distribute the zest and ginger.

2. Ladle into hot sterilized jars. Wipe the rims clean with a damp towel and seal with new lids and metal rings. Process in a hot-water bath (page 8) for 5 minutes. Remove, cool, check seals, label, and store.

POMEGRANATE JELLY

Try as I might, I could never bring this juice to a jellying point without the help of commercial pectin. Fortunately, pomegranate juice is tart enough to offset the large amount of sugar needed with it. And since it has enough acid, the jelly does not become a rubbery mass. It is a soft-set jelly, a startling magenta in color. Armenian and Middle Eastern markets carry bottled pomegranate juice.

Makes 7 half-pint jars

4 cups fresh or bottled
   pomegranate juice (about
   8 large pomegranates)
4 tablespoons fresh lemon juice

6 cups sugar
3 ounces commercial liquid
   pectin

1. To juice the pomegranates, cut the fruit in half through the stem end and press firmly over a reamer. Or remove the seeds with their surrounding sac and place in a processor. Pulse on and off quickly just enough to break up the juice from the seed. Strain into a measuring cup.

2. Combine the pomegranate juice, lemon juice, and sugar in a deep nonreactive saucepan or stockpot. Bring to a full boil, stirring. Pour in the pectin and bring to a boil again for 1 minute, stirring. Immediately remove from the heat and skim off foam.

3. Ladle into hot sterilized jars. Wipe the rims clean with a damp towel. Seal with new lids and metal rings. Process in a hot-water bath (page 8) for 5 minutes. Remove, cool, check seals, label, and store.

ROSE GERANIUM JELLY

Scented geraniums are numerous. Strangely, their fragrance and subsequent name come from the leaf rather than the flower. The aromatic property results from the leaves being covered with tiny glandular hairs called trichomes, which contain the scented oils. A gentle bruising will release their distinct aroma and, when grown indoors, they are a natural air freshener. The geranium belongs to a larger plant group called Pelargoniums, which are native to the Cape of Good Hope. They have been cultivated for over 300 years but it wasn't until the French discovered their potential as an ingredient in perfume in 1847 did they become well known. Usually grown as an annual, these varied-leaf and flowered plants are perennial in mild climates such as Southern California. Some of the scented-leaf geraniums available are Rose, Apricot, Hazelnut, Coconut, Green Apple, Ginger, Lemon (Citronella), Lemon-Rose, Lime, Nutmeg, Strawberry, Peach, Pine, and Peppermint. Each has a slightly different leaf and flower and is easily propagated.

Rose geranium jelly was made in England in Victorian times to be served with tea breads and scones. Highly fragrant, the taste of this jelly matches a buttery brioche, *pain de mie,* or warm scone perfectly. The intensity of flavor will vary with each jelly, since it is not always possible to obtain the variety of rose geranium with the most intensely scented leaf (Rober's Lemon Rose, which resembles a tomato plant). Make sure all leaves are pesticide-free.

Makes 6 half pint jars

4 cups fresh or bottled apple
  juice or cider
2 cups packed fresh rose
  geranium leaves, washed
5 cups sugar

2 tablespoons fresh lemon juice
3 ounces commercial liquid
  pectin
6 fresh pesticide-free rose
  geranium leaves for jars

1. Bring the apple juice and leaves to a boil in a large saucepan, cover, and remove from heat. Steep overnight at room temperature or as long as 3 days refrigerated.

2. Pour the juice through a strainer into a 4–6 quart deep saucepan. Press firmly on the leaves with the back of a spoon to extract as much flavor as possible, then discard. Stir in the sugar and lemon juice, and bring to a rolling boil over high heat, and boil for 5 minutes. Immediately pour in pectin and stir to combine. When mixture returns to a rolling boil again, start timing and continue cooking for 1 minute.

3. Remove from heat, skim foam, and ladle the jelly into hot sterilized jars, placing a fresh rose geranium leaf in each jar. Wipe rims clean with a damp towel. Seal with new lids and metal rings. Process in a hot-water bath (page 8) for 5 minutes. Remove, cool, check seals, label, and store. Leave jars undisturbed in a cool place for a week before using. This jelly continues to solidify for several days so do not be concerned if it does not look jelled immediately.

NUTMEG GERANIUM JELLY

Of all the scented geraniums, nutmeg is by far my favorite. With its delicate white flowers on long thin stems and small apple-green leaves, it makes a most pleasing potted plant. Brush against its highly aromatic foliage ever so gingerly, and the most intoxicating scent will be released. Even with my eyes closed while sunbathing on the deck, I can tell the dog is nearby because his tail has swatted the nutmeg geranium!

Makes 6 half-pint jars

4 cups fresh or bottled apple cider or juice

2 cups (packed) fresh nutmeg geranium leaves, washed

5 cups sugar

3 tablespoons fresh lemon juice

3 ounces liquid commercial pectin

1/4 teaspoon freshly grated nutmeg

6 fresh pesticide-free geranium leaves, washed, for jars

1. Bring the cider and leaves to a boil in a large saucepan. Cover, remove from the heat, and steep at room temperature overnight or as long as 3 days refrigerated.

2. The next day, pour the cider through a strainer into a 6- to 8-quart nonreactive saucepan. Press firmly on leaves to extract as much flavor as possible. Stir in the sugar and lemon juice and cook over high heat for 5 minutes. Stir in pectin and when mixture returns to a rolling boil, set timer to boil for 1 minute. Remove from heat, skim foam, and stir in the grated nutmeg.

3. Ladle into hot sterilized jars, placing a leaf in each jar; wipe the rims clean with a damp towel, and seal with new lids and metal rings. Process in a hot-water bath (page 8) for 5 minutes. Remove, cool, check seals, label, and store. Allow to cool to room temperature and store for 1 week before using. This jelly takes up to 48 hours to set completely.

ROSEMARY-MINT JELLY

Rosemary-mint jelly is wonderful on a warm rosemary biscuit when you are serving lamb. Be sure to pick extra sprigs of both herbs to put in the jars.

Makes 6 half-pint jars

3 1/2 cups fresh apple cider or
   bottled white grape juice
1 cup fresh rosemary needles
1 cup (packed) fresh mint leaves
4 cups sugar
1/2 cup rice wine vinegar

1 tablespoon fresh lemon juice
6 ounces commercial liquid
   pectin
6 sprigs fresh rosemary
6 sprigs fresh mint

1. Bring the cider, rosemary, and mint to a boil in a medium saucepan. Cover the pan and allow to steep overnight.

2. The next day, strain and discard the herbs. Add the sugar, vinegar, and lemon juice to the cider and bring to a boil. Stir in the pectin. Return to a full boil and cook for 1 minute. Turn off the heat.

3. Put a small sprig of each herb in each of 6 hot sterilized pint jars and ladle in the jelly. Wipe the rims clean with a damp towel and seal with new lids and metal rings. Process in a hot-water bath (page 8) for 5 minutes. Remove, cool, check seals, label, and store.

MEYER LEMON MARMALADE

Meyer lemons are worth asking around for. They have an infectious perfume that immediately distinguishes them from the common lemon. The flavor is sweeter, with a touch of orange, the skin very smooth and dark yellow. In California the Meyer lemon has two seasons a year, early spring and late fall. Primarily a "backyard" fruit, it can be found at local farmers' markets. Unfortunately, in this recipe the common lemon cannot be substituted. As with all citrus marmalades, allow two days for the preparation.

Makes 4 pint jars

20 Meyer lemons
Sugar

1. Remove the zest of 16 lemons with a zester. Or carefully cut it away with a paring knife, then slice the pieces into ⅛-inch strips. Reserve the remaining 4 lemons for juice. Place the zest in a large bowl.

2. With a paring knife, remove all but a very thin layer of the white pith and cut the fruit into quarters. Remove as many seeds as possible. Place the pulp in a food processor fitted with the metal blade and pulse until coarsely chopped. Measure the pulp and juices and add an equal amount of water. Pour the mixture into the bowl with the zest. Let stand at least 4 hours at room temperature or overnight, covered, in the refrigerator. *(continued)*

3. Pour the mixture into a shallow preserving pan and add the same amount of sugar as you did water in Step 2. Add the juice from the 4 remaining lemons. Stir and bring to a boil over moderately high heat. Scoop out any seeds. Cook for 30 minutes. The marmalade will look thin, but it continues to thicken as it cools.

4. Ladle into hot sterilized jars, wipe the rims clean with a damp towel, and seal with new lids and metal rings. Process in a hot-water bath (page 8) for 5 minutes. Remove, cool, check seals, label, and store.

CARAMELIZED APPLE MARMALADE WITH THYME

Whenever I want a really comforting winter dessert I make a *tarte Tatin* with warm, caramel-saturated apples on a crisp pastry crust. This marmalade expands the range of my favorite tart to include breakfast and the entree at dinner, on a warm apple bran muffin in the morning or alongside pork roast or glazed duck for dinner.

Makes 3 pint jars

10 large tart green apples, such as Granny Smith (about 4 pounds)

5 tablespoons fresh lemon juice

2 cups sugar

2 cups bottled or fresh apple juice

1 vanilla bean, split, scraped, and cut into thirds

1 teaspoon ground cinnamon

2 teaspoons finely chopped fresh thyme or 1 teaspoon dried thyme

1. Peel, core, and cut the apples into 1-inch pieces. Toss immediately in a large bowl with the lemon juice. Set aside.

2. Stir together the sugar, ½ cup of the apple juice, and the vanilla bean in a large nonreactive shallow preserving pan. Place over high heat and bring to a boil. Cool, without stirring, until the mixture caramelizes to a medium amber color. Add the apple slices and any accumulated juices, the remaining apple juice, cinnamon, and thyme. The caramel will clump together but will eventually remelt. Continue cooking on moderately high heat, watching carefully that the juices do not boil over. Turn the apples over in the syrup until the slices are completely glazed and translucent and there is little liquid left in the pan, about 20 to 30 minutes. Remove the vanilla bean. Some of the apples will break apart. Remove from the heat.

3. Spoon into hot sterilized jars, wipe the rims clean with a damp towel, and seal with new lids and metal rings. Process in a hot-water bath (page 8) for 5 minutes. Remove, cool, check seals, label, and store.

SPICED BLUEBERRY MARMALADE

There can never be too many blueberry recipes for me. Yet, when I tried to create a blueberry jam, I was disappointed. The color was there, of course, but the flavor was not. I found that adding citrus compensated for the lack of pectin in the berries and gave texture to the marmalade. Cinnamon provides a subtle spicy warmth.

Makes 5 half-pint jars

1 orange	*3 cups sugar*
1 lemon	*⅛ teaspoon ground cinnamon*
¼ cup fresh orange juice	*Dash of freshly grated nutmeg*
¼ cup fresh lemon juice	
4 cups fresh blueberries, washed and destemmed	

1. Cut a thin slice from each end of the orange and lemon and discard. Score through the peel in 4 places and gently remove. Lay each piece flat and cut away half of the white pith. Cut peel into very fine shreds, ⅛ inch by 1½ inches. Place the zest in a shallow pan with 1½ cups of water. Bring to a boil, cover, and cook on high heat for 10 minutes.

2. Meanwhile, remove the pulp of the orange and lemon from the membranes and add to peel. Squeeze membranes to extract any juice and add the orange and lemon juice. Cover and cook over medium heat for 15 minutes more. Add the blueberries, sugar, cinnamon,

and nutmeg to the citrus mixture. Bring the marmalade to a boil and continue cooking, uncovered, for 20 minutes. The blueberries will pop open and the mixture will begin to thicken slightly and appear glossy.

3. Turn off the heat and remove a small amount of marmalade to a saucer and place in the freezer for 5 minutes. If the mixture wrinkles as a whole (not just a skin on top) when pushed to one side with a finger, it is ready to be jarred. This jam will thicken a great deal as it cools, so avoid overcooking.

4. Ladle into hot sterilized jars, wipe the rims clean with a damp towel, and seal with new lids and metal rings. Process in a hot-water bath (page 8) for 5 minutes. Remove, cool, check seals, label, and store.

CANDIED GRAPEFRUIT PEEL MARMALADE

When I made grapefruit marmalade the traditional way by cutting the rind into strips and cooking it with the pulp of the fruit, the rind was far too bitter, even after repeated blanchings, so I tried using just the zest, which I like far better. Pink grapefruits make a lovely amber-colored jelly, but any variety that is sweet and full of juice is fine. Choose fruit that is heavy for its size since those will contain more juice.

Makes 4 half-pint jars

6 very large grapefruits
  (6 pounds)
2 cups sugar

1. Zest the outer skin only of 4 of the grapefruits with a zesting tool, saving 2 for juice. There should be 1 cup of zest. Bring 2 cups water and the sugar to a boil in a small saucepan and add the zest. Cook over moderately high heat, stirring occasionally, for 20 minutes, or until the zest looks translucent and has darkened in color. Remove from the heat.

2. Meanwhile, cut a thick slice off both ends of the 4 zested grape-fruit and discard. Stand the grapefruit on a cutting board and score the pith in 4 places vertically. Peel off as much of the white pith as possible. Holding the grapefruit over a bowl to catch any juices, carefully cut out the segments. Squeeze the juice from the remaining

membranes into the bowl and then discard. There should be about 4 cups of juice and pulp. Juice the reserved grapefruits, measure, and add enough water to make 2 cups if needed. Pour into the bowl. Pour in the zest and sugar syrup, stir, and let mixture stand 4 hours at room temperature or refrigerate overnight.

3. Bring the mixture to a boil over moderate heat in a large nonreactive shallow preserving pan and cook for 15 to 20 minutes, watching and stirring attentively. When the marmalade begins to look very foamy and bubbly on top, remove a small amount to a saucer. Place in the freezer for 5 minutes. If the mixture wrinkles when pushed to one side, it is ready. Citrus fruits have a lot of natural pectin and don't need excessive cooking to jell. The marmalade will thicken as it cools.

4. Ladle into hot sterilized jars, wipe rims clean with a damp towel, and seal with new lids and metal rings. Process in a hot-water bath (page 8) for 5 minutes. Remove, cool, check seals, label, and store.

CRANBERRY-RASPBERRY PRESERVES

Cranberries and raspberries certainly don't come into season together, but I like what they do for each other. The cranberries have a high pectin content, which the raspberries lack, and the color, texture, and flavor of the two are very compatible. You can buy cranberries in November and freeze them until raspberries are in season or buy frozen raspberries when the cranberries are fresh. Either way, begin this recipe with thawed fruit. This tart, bright red jam is perfect on warm cranberry-orange muffins. It also makes a spectacular topping for a Christmas cheesecake. Or serve it with your Thanksgiving turkey in place of a traditional cranberry relish.

Makes 4 pint jars

6 cups (3 pints) raspberries
2 1/2 cups sugar
3 cups cranberries (12-ounce bag)
1/4 cup fresh orange juice
grated zest of 1 orange

1. Stir together the raspberries and 1 cup of the sugar in a medium bowl and let stand for 1 hour.

2. Stir the cranberries and the remaining sugar together in a nonreactive shallow preserving pan and place over high heat. Stir constantly so the sugar does not burn until the cranberries begin to

release juice, about 5 minutes. Continue cooking until all the cranberries have popped and the mixture is syrupy and comes to a boil. Skim off any foam that forms on top and continue to cook and stir until the mixture thickens, about 10 minutes more.

3. Add the raspberries and all their juice and cook for 10 minutes more. Stir in the orange juice and zest.

4. Remove a small amount of the jam to a saucer and place in the freezer for 5 minutes. If the mixture wrinkles when pushed to one side, it is ready. If not, continue cooking for 5 minutes and retest.

5. When the preserves are the right consistency, turn down the heat to a simmer and ladle into hot sterilized jars. Wipe the rims clean with a damp towel and seal with new lids and metal rings. Process in a hot-water bath (page 8) for 5 minutes. Remove, cool, check seals, label, and store.

NECTARINE AND RASPBERRY PRESERVES

Because the raspberries are added at the very end of the cooking time, and cooked only very briefly with the nectarines, they retain their shape, color, and flavor.

Makes 8 half-pint jars

*6 pounds large nectarines,
   unpeeled and sliced (8 cups)
3 cups sugar*

*2 tablespoons fresh lemon juice
2 cups (1 pint) raspberries*

1. Combine the nectarines with the sugar and lemon juice and let stand, covered, overnight in the refrigerator.

2. Place a colander in a large shallow preserving pan and pour in the nectarine mixture. Let the juices drip into the pan for at least 30 minutes. Remove the colander with the fruit to a bowl and bring the juices in the pan to a boil over high heat. Boil rapidly for 20 to 30 minutes, or until reduced by half. Add the nectarines and any additional juices to the syrup in the pan and continue to cook over high heat for 10 minutes.

3. Carefully stir in the raspberries and cook for 5 minutes more. The nectarines will look lightly glazed and the syrup will be only slightly thickened.

4. Ladle the preserves into hot sterilized jars, wipe the rims clean with a damp towel, and seal with new lids and metal rings. Process in a hot-water bath (page 8) for 5 minutes. Remove, cool, check seals, label, and store.

PEACH PRESERVES

The method used in this recipe may be a bit more involved than some of the more traditional ones, but the results are worth it—chunks of tender fruit in a not-too-sweet, thickened syrup. Be sure to use a heavy-bottomed shallow pan so that evaporation can take place in the shortest time.

Makes 5 half-pint jars

6 to 7 pounds peaches, peeled   *2 cups sugar*
  and sliced (8 cups)   *2 tablespoons fresh lemon juice*

1. Toss the peaches with the sugar in a large bowl and let stand at room temperature for 2 to 3 hours, stirring occasionally. Place a large colander in a nonreactive shallow preserving pan. Pour the fruit and juice through the colander. Let drain for 15 minutes. Remove the colander with the fruit to a bowl.

2. Place the pan over high heat, add the lemon juice, and boil the juice into a syrup. It will look very foamy with small bubbles covering the entire surface. The time it takes will depend on how deep your pan is. Test with a candy thermometer; it should read 222° F. Immediately pour in the reserved fruit and juice. Cook over high heat just until the peaches appear caramelized around the edges. They will become more golden and look glazed.

3. Ladle into hot sterilized jars, wipe the rims clean with a damp towel, and seal with new lids and metal rings. Process in a hot-water bath (page 8) for 5 minutes. Remove, cool, check seals, label, and store.

WHOLE STRAWBERRY PRESERVES

Looking through cookbooks of the 1920s and 1930s I kept coming across a recipe for "Sun-cooked Strawberry Jam." How perfect— strawberries are in season just when the weather gets warm, the days grow longer, and the sun shines more often. Don't even be tempted to try this recipe unless you can find very red, very ripe, local (if possible) strawberries and the weatherman predicts at least three sunny days in a row. This jam is quickly prepared: no slicing the berries and only five minutes of cooking (on the stove, that is). Ah, but what you'll have is plump, really red, melt-in-your-mouth fruit surrounded by equally red, thick syrup, so delicious that once this jam is put into a jar, you'll never want to give it away. So, with that in mind, think *large* quantities when considering this recipe.

Makes 9 half-pint jars

12 pint baskets strawberries
5 cups sugar
3 tablespoons fresh lemon or
  lime juice

1. Rinse the berries briefly and drain. Remove stems and greens and any bruises. Toss the strawberries and sugar in a large nonreactive bowl and let stand at room temperature for 4 to 5 hours or refrigerate, covered, overnight. Stir frequently.

2. Pour the strawberry mixture into a large nonreactive deep pot and bring quickly to a boil over high heat. Stir in the lemon or lime juice and boil for 5 minutes. Watch closely as this could easily boil over. Turn off the heat and skim the foam. Carefully divide the mixture between two 11-inch by 15-inch jelly-roll pans, making sure each pan has the same amount of syrup. The berries should be at least half covered with syrup.

3. When cool enough to handle, carry the pans outside and place on a flat, steady surface in direct sun. Place fine mesh screening or an aluminum frame window screen over each pan. Every couple of hours, spoon some of the liquid over the berries to keep the tops moist. Bring the trays inside at night so they don't collect any moisture.

4. By the end of the third day in the sun, the liquid should just begin to wrinkle at the corners of the pan when a clean finger is drawn through the juices and be reduced by about half. If it hasn't thickened to that point, leave the pans out another day, continuing to baste the tops of the berries. The syrup should be a little thinner than you would want it, since it thickens when refrigerated.

5. Bring in the pans and pour the contents into a large deep pot and bring to a slow simmer. Immediately ladle the jam into hot sterilized jars, wipe the rims clean with a damp towel, and seal with new lids and metal rings. Process in a hot-water bath (page 8) for 5 minutes. Remove, cool, check seals, label, and store.

YELLOW TOMATO PRESERVES

Early one spring we started seeds for a miniature yellow pear-shaped tomato in the greenhouse. As is often the case with tomatoes, the yield from just three plants was far greater than one family's need. So I looked upon this plethora as yet another challenge. This savory and slightly piquante preserve is a perfect companion to warm corn-bread, a corn muffin, or rye toast. If the yellow pear-shaped tomato is unavailable, use another variety of yellow tomato and cut into 1-inch cubes. Red tomatoes don't make a good substitute here for the sweeter, less acidic yellow ones.

Makes 4 half-pint jars

4 cups sugar

5 cups very small pear-shaped
  yellow tomatoes

3 fresh jalapeño chilies, seeded
  and minced

3 tablespoons finely chopped
  fresh basil leaves

3 tablespoons fresh lemon juice

1. In a 4- to 6-quart heavy nonreactive shallow preserving pan, stir together the sugar and ¾ cup water. Set over medium heat and bring to a boil. Wash down any sugar crystals that accumulate on the sides of the pan with a pastry brush dipped in cold water.

2. Insert a candy thermometer and continue boiling until the syrup has reached 234° F, the soft-ball stage.

3. Immediately stir in tomatoes. The mixture will seize but after a few minutes will again become liquid. Stir in the chilies, basil, and lemon juice and turn heat to very low. Continue simmering for 3 hours, stirring occasionally. The mixture will have thickened and darkened in color.

4. Ladle into hot, sterilized jars, wipe rims clean with a damp towel, and seal with new lids and metal rings. Process in a hot-water bath (page 8) for 10 minutes. Preserves will continue to thicken as they cool. Remove, cool, check seals, label, and store.

APRICOTS IN ORANGE-HONEY SYRUP

Preserved apricots certainly don't measure up to fresh-off-the-tree ones, but these are delicious and very versatile. Placed next to a small scoop of vanilla ice cream and drizzled with their own syrup, they are an elegant instant dessert. They also go with roast duck or chicken or can be teamed up with winter fruits in a warm compote. Choose unblemished and firm small apricots so more can be wedged into a jar.

Makes 2 pint jars

1 small orange

1 ½ cups sugar

*2 pounds small apricots
 (16 to 20)*

2 tablespoons honey

¼ teaspoon almond extract

*2 cinnamon sticks, about
 2 inches each*

1. Cut a thin slice from each end of the orange. With a sharp knife, make 4 vertical cuts through the peel to score it. Pull off the peel. Cut away most of the pith and slice the zest into ¼-inch strips. Set aside. Squeeze the juice from the orange; you should have ¼ cup.

2. Combine the sugar and 1¾ cups water in a medium saucepan and bring to a boil over high heat. Add the orange zest and juice. Continue boiling for 15 minutes.

3. Add the apricots and simmer for 5 minutes. Stir in the honey and almond extract.

4. Remove the apricots with a slotted spoon to 2 hot sterilized widemouthed pint jars, wedging them in as tight as possible. Squeeze a cinnamon stick into each jar. Bring the syrup to a boil and pour over the fruit, filling to within ½ inch of the top.

5. Wipe the rims of the jars clean with a damp towel. Seal with new lids and metal rings and process in a hot-water bath (page 8) for 15 minutes. Remove and let cool. Season for 4 weeks before using. Check seals, label, and store.

SPICED PEACHES WITH VANILLA BEAN

My grandmother and mother pickled peaches every summer. The cinnamon-colored fruit would encircle a roast chicken, duck, or ham. When I began cooking for my own family, I realized they were missing from my own pantry, and I had never seen any for sale. And so I've continued the family tradition.

Jarring up whole peaches takes much less labor than preparing them for jam. With their blush-pink cheeks pressed against the sides of a quart Mason jar, these wonderful peaches suspended in a vanilla-flecked syrup make a spectacular gift if you can bear to part with them. Choose a medium (3 to 4 to the pound), firm but ripe, freestone variety peach. The freestone allows for much easier eating than the cling and often has a better color.

Makes 2 quart jars

4 1/2 pounds freestone peaches (about 14)

4 cups sugar

3 1/2 cups champagne or white wine vinegar

4 cinnamon sticks, about 2 inches each

12 whole allspice berries

8 whole cloves

2 vanilla beans

1. Score a very small **X** through the skin on the bottom of each peach. Drop into boiling water and cook for 3 minutes. Remove to a colander to drain and cool. Starting at the **X**, peel the skin away without marring the flesh. Set the peeled peaches aside. Handle gently.

2. Combine the sugar, champagne or vinegar, cinnamon sticks, allspice, and cloves in a large pot. Cut the vanilla beans in half lengthwise and scrape the seeds into the pot. Reserve the beans. Simmer, uncovered, for 20 minutes. Carefully add the peaches and continue to cook on medium heat for 15 minutes, basting with liquid if the peaches are not totally immersed.

3. Turn off the heat and remove the peaches with a slotted spoon to hot sterilized widemouthed quart jars. Pack the fruit in as tight as possible without crushing or mashing. Cut a peach in half, leaving the pit intact in one half, if necessary to fill the jar. Slide 2 cinnamon sticks and 1 vanilla bean into each jar. Put 6 allspice berries and 4 cloves in each jar. Pour boiling syrup over the fruit, filling the jars to within ½ inch of the top.

4. Wipe the rims of the jars clean with a damp towel and seal with new lids and metal rings. Process in a hot-water bath (page 8) for 15 minutes. Remove, cool, check seals, and label before storing. Season for 4 weeks before using. The peaches will darken slightly over time.

CLEMENTINES OR NAVEL ORANGES IN SYRUP MANDARINE

What a dignified dessert! I can visualize three perfect little oranges settled in a shallow glass dish bathing contentedly in a silky custard sauce. A quart of these also makes a very thoughtful hostess gift at holiday time, but don't give them all away. The inspiration for preserving clementines came from an abundant crop shared by my husband's parents, Mary and Ralph Waycott. I was intent on finding a way to prolong their fresh, tart taste and still be able to appreciate their appealing diminutive size.

Makes 3 quart jars

6 pounds clementines,
   mandarins, or very small
   navel oranges
2 cups fresh orange juice
1 cup fresh lemon juice
3 cups sugar
1/2 cup honey

1 cinnamon stick, 3 inches long
6 whole cloves
5 whole allspice berries
1/4 cup Napoleon Mandarine
   liqueur or other
   orange-flavored liqueur

1. Carefully remove the peel and white fibers from the clementines without breaking the fruit. Set aside.

2. Combine the orange juice, lemon juice, sugar, honey, and 4 cups of water in a large saucepan. Tie the cinnamon stick, cloves, and allspice in a small piece of cheesecloth and add to the sugar mixture. Boil for 5 minutes to dissolve the sugar.

3. Add the fruit to the boiling syrup and continue cooking for 20 minutes. Remove from the heat, cover pan, and let the fruit stand in the syrup overnight at room temperature.

4. The next day, bring the mixture back to a boil. Gently remove the fruit with a slotted spoon and place in hot sterilized widemouthed quart jars. Continue boiling the syrup until slightly reduced, about 15 minutes. Remove the spice bag and discard. Stir in liqueur. Pour hot syrup over the oranges, filling the jars to within ½ inch of the top.

5. Seal with new lids and metal rings. Process in a hot-water bath (page 8) for 15 minutes. Remove and let cool. Check seals, label, and store.

MANGO CHUTNEY

Chunky mango chutney that isn't overly sweet is hard to find. This one goes with Indian curries and simple barbecued chicken, and a couple of tablespoonfuls make a wild rice salad sprinkled with pine nuts or almonds into a refreshing summer dish.

Makes 6 pint jars

8 large mangoes, peeled and cut into ¹/₂-inch (about ¹/₂ pound each) strips (pages 26–27)

2 cups cider vinegar

2 cups granulated sugar

1 cup dark brown sugar

2 large onions, finely chopped

6 cloves garlic, minced

3 teaspoons coarsely ground black pepper

¹/₂ teaspoon salt

¹/₂ teaspoon cayenne

1 tablespoon ground cinnamon

1 tablespoon finely minced gingerroot

¹/₂ teaspoon ground cloves

1 teaspoon ground allspice

2 teaspoons whole mustard seeds

1 cup raisins

2 large tart green apples, peeled, cored, and finely chopped

1. Combine all the ingredients in a large bowl, cover, and let stand overnight in the refrigerator.

2. The next day, pour the mixture into a large shallow nonreactive preserving pan and bring to a boil, uncovered. Reduce the heat and simmer until very syrupy, about 30 minutes.

3. Ladle into hot sterilized jars to within ½ inch of the top and wipe the rims clean with a damp towel. Seal with new lids and metal rings. Process in a hot-water bath (page 8) for 10 minutes. Remove and let cool. Check seals, label, and store. Season for 3 weeks before using.

FRUIT BUTTERS, SYRUPS, AND SAUCES

uch more than just jams and jellies can be made from fresh fruit. Fruit butters are the result of long, slow cooking that reduces a puree into a butterlike consistency with concentrated fruit flavor. It is not a process recommended for fruits with a high proportion of water like berries or melons. Although pure maple syrup is hard to beat on pancakes or waffles, it is nice to know that a concentrated fruit syrup is a snap to make. Commercial fruit-flavored syrups are far too sweet and lack a real fruit identity. Use these syrups for the basis of a milk shake or stir a tablespoon into yogurt. Knowing there is a jar of fruit-based sauce in the pantry can give you peace of mind that an instant dessert is close at hand. Sauces can excite the most mundane of components: ice cream, pound cake, crepes, or a peach half.

PEACH BUTTER

I certainly didn't invent peach butter; recipes for such have been around for decades. My recipe actually evolved from overcooking peach jam. After all the chunks had dissolved into puree, I decided to continue cooking the mixture in the oven to further thicken it. What resulted was an intensely flavored spread with the consistency of soft butter. Spoonful for spoonful there was a very high concentration of flavor, even though the texture of the peach had been lost to pureeing. This is one recipe where doubling the recipe will not affect the chemistry. The cooking time will be longer, but as long as you watch carefully the end product will be just as delicious.

Makes 4 pint jars

10 to 12 pounds ripe peaches, peeled and cut into 1/3-inch slices (about 16 cups)

3 cups sugar

2 tablespoons fresh lemon juice

1/4 teaspoon almond extract

1/4 teaspoon freshly grated nutmeg

1. Stir all the ingredients together in a large nonreactive shallow preserving pan. Let stand at room temperature for 4 hours.

2. Place the pan over high heat and bring the mixture to a boil. Lower the heat to moderate and cook, stirring occasionally, for 20 minutes, or until peaches appear glazed and are soft.

3. Preheat the oven to 225° F.

4. Pour the contents in batches into a food processor fitted with the metal blade, and puree. Pour the puree into a bowl while processing the remaining batches. Pour the puree into the preserving pan if ovenproof, or into a shallow roasting pan and place in the oven. Stir every 30 minutes for 2 to 3 hours. The puree will turn dark amber and become very thick. It will tend to darken more rapidly around the edges of the pan, so be sure to thoroughly stir.

5. Remove from the oven and pour into hot sterilized jars. Wipe the rims clean with a damp towel. Seal with new lids and metal rings. Process in a hot-water bath (page 8) for 10 minutes. Remove, cool, check seals, label, and store.

APPLE CIDER BUTTER

Nearly every old cookbook has a recipe for apple butter, but not many modern ones do. Is it too old-fashioned? Too boring? No and no again. What it does take is time to get a thick-as-sludge, intense, apple-flavored, spiced spread. The type of apple doesn't seem to make a great deal of difference in flavor; it's just a question of how sweet the apple is and therefore how much sugar is needed. Apple butter is definitely a winter taste so take advantage of the abundance of apples next fall and pack some apple butter away to put in your Christmas gift baskets.

Makes 6 pint jars

7 to 8 pounds apples, tart, green (Granny Smith, pippin), washed and quartered but unpeeled

6 cups apple cider, fresh or bottled

3 cups sugar

1 teaspoon ground cinnamon

1/4 teaspoon ground allspice

1/4 teaspoon ground cloves

dash freshly grated nutmeg

1. Combine the apples, 4 cups of the cider, and 4 cups of water in a large stockpot. Bring to a boil over high heat and cook until the apples are very soft, about 20 minutes. Remove from the heat and cool slightly.

2. Puree the apples in a food mill in batches, discarding the seeds and peel. Transfer to an ovenproof pan and stir in the remaining cider, the sugar, cinnamon, allspice, cloves, and nutmeg.

3. Place the pan over moderate heat and bring to a simmer, stirring occasionally. Reduce the heat to low and cook for 3 hours, uncovered, stirring frequently to prevent scorching.

4. Preheat the oven to 250° F.

5. Place the pan on the center rack of the oven. Cook for 8 hours, stirring about once an hour, scraping the sides of the pan. The color will darken and a skin will form between stirrings.

6. Remove a tablespoonful to a small saucer. Chill for 5 minutes in the freezer. The chilled mixture should be thick enough to mound and not slide from the spoon. Taste and adjust the sugar and spices if necessary. Continue cooking for 3 to 4 hours more.

7. Fill the jars. If you do not wish to jar the apple butter at this time, cover and refrigerate for up to 3 days. Then bring to a boil on top of the stove and ladle into hot sterilized jars. Wipe the rims clean with a damp towel, and seal with new lids and metal rings. Process in a hot-water bath (page 8) for 10 minutes. Remove, cool, check seals, label, and store.

POMEGRANATE PANCAKE SYRUP

Pancakes are probably the most popular weekend breakfast treat, certainly in my house. Looking for a new syrup taste, I tried to duplicate the consistency of maple syrup with a fruit juice. With a pomegranate tree in the front yard, I didn't have to look far. (See page 45 for how to make fresh juice.) Bottled pomegranate juice also works; it can be found in Armenian and Middle Eastern markets. Cooking the juice down resulted in a syrup that goes well with buckwheat and blueberry pancakes.

Makes 1 pint jar

*4 cups pomegranate juice,
    bottled or fresh (12 large
    pomegranates)*
¾ cup sugar
1 tablespoon fresh lemon juice

1. Bring the juice to a boil over high heat in a medium nonreactive saucepan and cook until it is reduced by half, approximately 20 minutes. Reduce the heat to a simmer and stir in the sugar and lemon juice. Cook for 5 minutes to dissolve sugar.

2. Pour into a hot sterilized pint jar and seal with a new lid and metal ring. Process in a hot-water bath (page 8) for 5 minutes. Remove, cool, check seals, label, and store. Syrup will also keep refrigerated for 2 weeks.

CRANBERRY KETCHUP

Well, what else do you put on a turkey sandwich? Use this thick red sauce on other poultry as well.

Makes 2 pint jars

*4 cups cranberries (about two
  12-ounce bags)*
1 1/2 cups red wine vinegar
4 whole allspice berries

8 whole cloves
1 cinnamon stick, 3 inches
2 cups brown sugar

1. Stir together the cranberries, vinegar, and 1 1/2 cups of water in a large nonreactive saucepan. Tie the allspice, cloves, and cinnamon together in a small piece of cheesecloth and add to the pan. Bring to a boil, lower the heat to medium, and cook until the cranberries have popped and are tender.

2. Remove and discard the spice bag and press the cranberries with a metal spoon through a strainer. Discard the skins. Return the pulp to the saucepan and stir in sugar. Boil until the sugar is dissolved and the sauce thickened, about 10 minutes.

3. Ladle into hot sterilized jars, wipe the rims clean with a damp towel, and seal with new lids and metal rings. Process in a hot-water bath (page 8) for 10 minutes. Remove, cool, check seals, label, and store.

MULLED WINE–BLUEBERRY SAUCE

That ski lodge favorite, hot mulled wine, is the basis for this made-in-summer fruit sauce. It can be spooned over buckwheat pancakes, half a peach filled with ice cream, or fruit shortcake.

You can use a commercial mixture of whole spices called mulled wine spices or mulling spices instead of my selection. Substitute 2 tablespoons of the ready-made for ones in this recipe. But include zest and lemon juice.

Makes 3 pint jars

*1 bottle (750 ml.) red wine or
  3 ³/₄ cups*

2 teaspoons whole peppercorns

*2 teaspoons whole allspice
  berries*

*2 vanilla beans, split and
  scraped, or 2 tablespoons
  vanilla extract*

Zest of 1 lemon

1 tablespoon fresh lemon juice

*3 cinnamon sticks, about
  3 inches each*

*¹/₄ teaspoon freshly grated
  nutmeg*

*4 cups fresh blueberries, washed
  and destemmed*

²/₃ cup sugar

1. Pour the wine into a large skillet over high heat. Add the peppercorns, allspice, vanilla, lemon zest, lemon juice, cinnamon sticks, and nutmeg. Bring to a boil and cook over high heat until the wine is reduced to 2 cups, about 15 minutes. Strain and return to the pan.

2. Add the blueberries and sugar. Bring to a boil again, reduce the heat, and cook just until the berries pop.

3. Ladle into hot sterilized jars, wipe the rims clean with a damp towel, and seal with new lids and metal rings. Process in a hot-water bath (page 8) for 5 minutes. Remove, cool, check seals, label, and store. The sauce will also keep in the refrigerator, covered, for 4 days.

PICKLED AND PRESERVED
VEGETABLES

*P*ickling is one of the oldest known methods of preserving food, dating back to biblical times. Either a salt brine or vinegar solution can be used. Pickled vegetables can also be fresh-packed and sealed in vacuum jars, then given a hot-water bath. Ideally vegetables to be preserved should be picked fresh from the garden and kept in the refrigerator until ready for preparation. They should be uniform in size so the reaction to the brine or pickling solution is consistent. Ingredients for relishes or salsas need to be chopped into pieces of equal size. To ensure preservation, vinegar with a 5 percent acidity is preferable. Cider, champagne, or wine vinegars are mellow and give a nice blending of flavors, but may darken white or light-colored vegetables such as onions, turnips, and white asparagus. Distilled vinegar has a sharp, pungent flavor that can be balanced with a little sugar; it is the one to use when a colorless pickling liquid is needed.

Salt used for pickling or preserving should be pure. Pickling salt, which is sold in 5-pound bags at some supermarkets, is preferred. When that is unavailable, kosher salt is the next best. Iodized salt and table salt and sea salt are undesirable because they contain additives that may discolor or cloud the brine.

Spices and herbs are additional flavor-makers. They too are always best when fresh and whole, but dried herbs can be used. Commercially prepared pickling spice blends can be found in the spice section of supermarkets. These and other spices can be tied up in a small muslin or cheesecloth bag for easy removal and heated with the vinegar, or they can be added loose to the pickling solution.

PICKLED BABY TURNIPS

Snow-white, buttery baby turnips the size of radishes are mellow tasting and tender when preserved in mild rice vinegar. Leaving a small amount of greenery on the stem and packing the jar with some turnip greens add visual interest.

Makes 2 pint jars

6 bunches baby turnips, about
   1 inch in diameter, including
   greens (about 40)

1 1/3 cups rice wine vinegar

4 tablespoons sugar

1 teaspoon kosher or pickling
   salt

20 whole peppercorns, cracked

1. Trim the stems and greens to within 1/2 inch of each turnip. Scrub well and remove taproot. Reserve 1/2 cup of the smallest greens from the center of the bunches.

2. Heat together the vinegar, 1 cup of water, the sugar, salt, and peppercorns in a small nonreactive saucepan. Simmer while cooking the turnips.

3. Cook the turnips in boiling salted water for 5 minutes. Drain and divide equally between 2 widemouthed pint jars that have been sterilized and kept hot. Insert the reserved greens along the sides of the jars. Pour in the hot vinegar mixture to within 1/2 inch of the top.

4. Wipe the rims clean with a damp towel and seal with new lids and metal rings. Process in a hot-water bath (page 8) for 15 minutes. Remove, cool, check seals, label, and store. Season for 2 weeks before using.

PICKLED BABY BEETS AND RASPBERRIES

I love red. So, for me, beets, raspberries, and raspberry vinegar naturally come together to add an intense accent to a plate of marinated vegetables. Cradled in a tender leaf of butter lettuce and drizzled with extra-virgin olive oil, this sweet-sour combo becomes an instant salad, ideal for Christmas dinner.

Makes 2 pint jars

1 pound miniature beets, no more than 1 1/2 inches in diameter (about 20)

1/2 cup sugar

2 cups raspberry vinegar

2 teaspoons whole allspice berries

1 cinnamon stick, about 3 inches long, broken in half

1 teaspoon kosher or pickling salt

1 cup fresh raspberries

1. Cut the green tops off the beets, leaving 1 inch of stem. Scrub well and trim taproot. Cook in boiling water for 5 minutes until crisp-tender. Plunge into cold water to stop cooking.

2. Combine the sugar, vinegar, 1 cup of water, the allspice, cinnamon, and salt in a nonreactive medium saucepan and simmer for 15 minutes.

3. Pack the beets and raspberries into 2 hot sterilized widemouthed pint jars and pour in the boiling liquid to within ½ inch of the top. Evenly distribute the spices between the jars.

4. Wipe the rims clean with a damp towel and seal with new lids and metal rings. Process in a hot-water bath (page 8) for 15 minutes. Remove, cool, check seals, label, and store. Season for 2 weeks before using.

PICKLED JERUSALEM ARTICHOKE

Those mysterious, bumpy, gingerlike knobs in the produce area make delicious, crunchy pickles. The Jerusalem artichoke, or sunchoke, is related neither to Jerusalem nor to artichokes. It is a tuber that some culinary historians claim is one of the very few indigenous American vegetables. Although available all year, they are best and sweetest during the fall and winter months. To retain their characteristic crunch and clean, white color, soak them in brine overnight.

Makes 4 pint jars

3 pounds Jerusalem artichokes
2 cups kosher or pickling salt
4 cups white wine vinegar
1 cup sugar
1 tablespoon whole black peppercorns

2 tablespoons whole mustard seeds
2 teaspoons celery seed
1/2 teaspoon crushed red pepper
1/2 cup finely chopped onion

1. Scrub the Jerusalem artichokes well with a stiff brush and cut into 1-inch chunks. There should be about 2 quarts. Stir together 8 cups of water and the salt in a large bowl. Add the artichoke pieces and soak overnight at room temperature.

2. The next day, drain the artichokes and rinse well. Bring the vinegar and sugar to a boil in a large nonreactive saucepan. Add the peppercorns, mustard seed, celery seed, red pepper, and onion. Lower the heat to a simmer while filling the jars.

3. Tightly pack the artichokes into 4 hot sterilized jars. Immediately pour the hot vinegar mixture over the artichokes, filling the jars to within ½ inch of the top. Make sure to evenly distribute the seasonings among the jars.

4. Wipe the rims clean with a damp towel. Seal with new lids and metal rings and process in a hot-water bath (page 8) for 15 minutes. Remove the jars to a wire rack, cool, check seals, label, and store. Season for 6 weeks before using.

PENCIL ASPARAGUS IN GARLIC VINEGAR

Even though I find it hard to imagine ever getting tired of eating asparagus, I suppose there may come a time. Although preserved asparagus never seem to retain the color of the fresh, the taste and texture can certainly be preserved. Pulling these delectable stalks out in the middle of winter, sieving a hard-cooked egg over the top, drizzling with olive oil, you have a salad anyone would envy. Choose the thinnest asparagus available; the thicker stalks just don't stay as tender when preserved. My ever helpful and solicitous editor, Harriet, says that she actually picks an abundance of asparagus in upstate New York and would delight in one more way to serve it. Here's to Harriet!

Makes 2 quart jars

3 pounds asparagus, as thin as possible

3 cups rice wine vinegar

2 teaspoons kosher or pickling salt

4 tablespoons sugar

2 teaspoons commercial pickling spices

1/4 teaspoon coarsely ground black pepper

4 garlic cloves, thinly sliced

1. Lay the asparagus on a cutting board with the tips all at one end. Trim the stalks to within 1 inch of the height of a widemouthed quart jar. Carefully insert asparagus tightly into 2 hot sterilized jars.

2. Combine the vinegar, 3 cups of water, the salt, sugar, pickling spices, pepper, and garlic in a nonreactive medium saucepan and heat just to a boil. Pour over the asparagus to within ½ inch of the top of each jar, distributing the garlic and seasonings as evenly as possible.

3. Wipe the rims clean with a damp towel and seal with new lids and metal rings. Process in a hot-water bath (page 8) for 15 minutes. Remove, cool, check seals, label, and store. Season for 1 month before using.

PICKLED BABY OKRA PODS

While other baby vegetables have recently become popular, pickled baby okra have been around for some time. My mother has been making these every year for as long as I can remember. Check her pantry, I can bet there is at least one jar in there right now.

Makes 6 pint jars

6 teaspoons dillseed

3 pounds very small okra pods, 1½ to 2 inches long, washed and patted dry

12 small garlic cloves, peeled

6 dried red chili peppers

3 small jalapeño peppers, cut in half and seeds removed

1 quart distilled white vinegar

½ cup kosher or pickling salt

1. Sprinkle ½ teaspoon of the dillseed into each of 6 widemouthed sterilized pint jars. Tightly wedge in the okra, stem end up. Squeeze 2 garlic cloves, 1 red pepper, and ½ jalapeño pepper into each jar.

2. Bring the vinegar, salt, and 1 cup of water to a boil in a medium nonreactive saucepan. Pour over the okra, filling to within ½ inch of the top of each jar. Sprinkle the top of each jar with the remaining dillseed.

3. Wipe the rims clean with a damp towel. Seal the jars with new lids and metal rings and process in a hot-water bath (page 8) for 10 minutes. Remove, cool, check seals, label, and store. Season for 6 weeks before using.

HARICOTS VERTS PRESERVED WITH GARLIC AND BASIL

If *haricots verts* can't be found, the thinnest of young string beans can be used.

Makes 2 pint jars

1 pound haricots verts

6 large basil leaves

2 garlic cloves, thinly sliced

1½ cups champagne vinegar or white wine vinegar

½ teaspoon kosher or pickling salt

¼ teaspoon coarsely ground black pepper

1. Trim the beans to fit within 1 inch of the top of a widemouthed pint jar. Cook the beans in boiling salted water for 3 minutes. Remove and plunge into a bowl filled with ice water to stop cooking and cool rapidly. Drain and divide the beans into 2 equal batches.

2. Lay a hot sterilized widemouthed pint jar on its side and fill halfway with beans. Place 3 of the basil leaves and half of the garlic on the beans. Continue adding beans, wedging tightly, until one of the batches is used. Repeat with the second jar.

3. Bring the vinegar, 1½ cups of water, the salt, and pepper to a boil in a nonreactive small saucepan. Stand the jars upright and fill to within ½ inch of the top.

4. Wipe the rims clean with a damp towel. Seal with new lids and metal rings. Process in a hot-water bath (page 8) for 15 minutes. Remove, cool, check seals, label, and store. Season for at least 4 weeks before using.

PRESERVED MINIATURE ZUCCHINI

Those cute little squash that look as though they would be a perfect portion for a dollhouse dinner can be seasoned with a tangy vinegar solution and turned into a marinated vegetable.

Makes 2 pint jars

1 1/4 pounds miniature zucchini, about 3 inches long (55 to 65)

4 sprigs fresh thyme

3/4 cup white wine vinegar

2 tablespoons kosher or pickling salt

2 tablespoons sugar

4 garlic cloves, thinly sliced

2 teaspoons commercial pickling spices

1. Scrub the zucchini with a vegetable brush. Trim from the stem end to fit within 1/2 inch of the top of a widemouthed pint jar. Lay 2 hot sterilized widemouthed pint jars on their sides and place zucchini in, stem end up, along the sides of the jars, wedging them in as tightly as possible. Turn the jars right side up and insert 2 sprigs of thyme into each.

2. Heat together the vinegar, 3/4 cup of water, the salt, sugar, garlic, and pickling spices in a nonreactive medium saucepan just to a boil. Pour the vinegar mixture to within 1/2 inch of the top of each jar.

3. Wipe the rims clean with a damp towel. Seal with new lids and metal rings. Process in a hot-water bath (page 8) for 15 minutes. Remove, cool, check seals, label, and store. Season for 2 weeks before using.

MARINATED BABY SUNBURST SQUASH

When these bright yellow pattypan squash, shaped like old-fashioned spinning tops, appear people are bound to smile. Their diminutive size and dazzling sunshine color are most appealing. If you see some in the market grab an extra pound and pack them into a tangy marinade to perk up a dinner in the doldrums of winter.

Makes 2 pint jars

1 pound miniature sunburst pattypan squash (about 40)
1 cup white wine vinegar
1/2 cup olive oil
2 cloves garlic

1 tablespoon kosher or pickling salt
1 tablespoon sugar
2 teaspoons commercial pickling spices

1. Wash the squash and wedge as tightly as possible into 2 hot sterilized widemouthed pint jars.

2. Heat together the vinegar, 1 cup of water, the oil, garlic, salt, sugar, and pickling spices in a nonreactive medium saucepan. Stir to dissolve the salt and sugar. Bring just to a boil and pour it over the squash to within 1/2 inch of the top of the jars, distributing the garlic and spices as evenly as possible.

3. Wipe the rims clean with a damp towel. Seal with new lids and metal rings. Process in a hot-water bath (page 8) for 15 minutes. Remove, cool, check seals, label, and store. Season for 2 weeks before using.

BABY CARROTS IN HONEY, VINEGAR, AND DILL

Baby carrots are scrumptious. Peeling is unnecessary; it removes a fine layer of nutrition. If you are lucky enough to have sandy or loamy soil do plant your own carrots in the early spring. Well-drained soil is necessary for very straight, well-formed carrots, and their germination period is short. Pull them when the green tops are about 12 inches high. Often the pride of a child's first garden vegetable, these sweet, tender carrots will be hard to resist nibbling. Preserving the natural crunch of baby carrots and enhancing their innate mellowness are what this recipe strives to do. Packing them into jars just after they are blanched ensures that they will be crisp when you retrieve a jar from the pantry next winter.

Makes 2 pint jars

1 pound baby carrots, about 3 1/2 inches long	*1/4 teaspoon ground white pepper*
1 cup white wine vinegar	*3 tablespoons honey*
2 teaspoons kosher or pickling salt	*4 sprigs fresh young dill*

1. Trim the greens to within 1 inch of the carrot tops. Scrub the carrots, using a vegetable brush. Trim the carrots at the root end to fit within 1/2 inch of the top of a widemouthed jar. Blanch the

carrots in boiling water for 2 minutes and drain. Wedge tightly into 2 hot sterilized widemouthed pint jars, turning some upside down if necessary.

2. Combine the vinegar, 1 cup of water, the salt, pepper, and honey in a nonreactive small saucepan and bring just to a boil. Pour over the carrots, filling the jars to within $\frac{1}{2}$ inch of the top. There may be liquid left over. Insert 2 sprigs of dill into each jar.

3. Wipe the rims clean with a damp towel. Seal with new lids and metal rings. Process in a hot-water bath (page 8) for 15 minutes. Remove, cool, check seals, label, and store. Season for 2 weeks before using.

ROASTED PEPPERS AND EGGPLANT IN GARLIC-CHILI OIL

Roasted peppers and eggplant are a combination that appears frequently in recipes or on menus. Sandwiched between pasta in lasagna, strewn over a pizza crust, included in an antipasto platter, or simply spread on an olive oil-brushed baguette for a sandwich, these compatible partners form beautiful striations in a canning jar. Take advantage of the late-summer seasonal overlap of peppers and Japanese eggplant (although small globe eggplants can be substituted). Both seem to be more or less available almost all year, but prices can double during the winter.

Makes 2 pint jars

4 large red bell peppers

2 large yellow bell peppers

5 medium Japanese eggplants or 3 small globe eggplants, no more than 2 1/2 inches in diameter

1 cup olive oil

2 cloves garlic, thinly sliced

1/4 teaspoon crushed red pepper

1/2 teaspoon kosher or pickling salt

8 to 10 large basil leaves

1. Place the peppers on a rimmed baking sheet. Lightly oil a second baking sheet. Slice the eggplant crosswise 1/3 inch thick and lay on the oiled baking sheet. Broil the peppers and eggplant about 4 inches from the heat. As the peppers become charred, rotate them carefully with tongs. The longer and slower the broiling, the more flavor the peppers will have. Turn the eggplant slices with a spatula when the

tops become lightly browned. The peppers should take about 30 minutes; the eggplant, 15 to 20 minutes. Remove the peppers to a plastic or brown paper bag and allow to steam until cool enough to handle. Remove from the bag, pull out the stems and any attached seeds, and cut the peppers into quarters lengthwise. Gently peel away the transparent outer skin and remove any additional seeds on the inside. Set aside.

2. Heat the oil, garlic, and red pepper and salt in a small saucepan. Simmer for 5 minutes.

3. Layer pepper strips, eggplant slices, and basil leaves in 2 hot sterilized widemouthed pint jars, drizzling each layer with a little of the hot oil. Press down firmly on the vegetables to pack tightly into the jars. Pour in the remaining oil to within 1/2 inch of the top.

4. Wipe the rims clean with a damp towel. Seal with new lids and metal rings. Process in a hot-water bath (page 8) for 15 minutes. Remove, cool, check seals, label, and store. Season for at least 2 weeks before using.

MARINATED MUSHROOM MÉLANGE

Have you noticed how many varieties of mushrooms are in the produce section now? Shiitakes, oysters, morels, crimini, hedgehogs, and porcini—they have subtle taste differences but can successfully be combined in a vinaigrette. Even more varied in shape than in flavor, these sometimes flamboyant (golden chanterelles) and sometimes mysterious (black trumpets) fungi need only light sautéing to become tender and absorb a garlicky herbal coating. Wild mushrooms should never be cleaned under running water. Gently scrub them with a vegetable brush or wipe carefully with a dampened paper towel. If dirt remains embedded, use a small knife to scrape it away. Mushrooms have a high content of water, which exudes during cooking. Keep them on low heat and when the juice has evaporated they should be done. These make a delicious first course nestled in a leaf of radicchio or as part of an antipasto platter.

Makes 2 pint jars

2 pounds mushrooms, mixed or all small button mushrooms

3 tablespoons plus ¾ cup extra-virgin olive oil

3 cloves garlic, minced

2 shallots, minced

2 tablespoons white wine vinegar

¼ cup balsamic vinegar

1 tablespoon chopped fresh marjoram

1 tablespoon chopped fresh sage or 1 teaspoon dried sage

2 tablespoons chopped flat-leaf parsley

½ teaspoon kosher or pickling salt

1. Wipe all the mushrooms clean with a damp towel. If very large, cut in half.

2. Heat 3 tablespoons of the olive oil in a 12-inch skillet over medium heat and add the mushrooms. Reduce the heat to low and gently sauté until all are tender, about 10 minutes. With a slotted spoon, remove the mushrooms to a bowl.

3. Turn the heat back to medium and add the garlic, shallots, and vinegars. Cook, stirring, until soft, about 10 minutes. Add the herbs and the remaining olive oil and salt. When the oil is hot, return the mushrooms to the pan and heat through, tossing with the herb mixture. Divide the mushrooms and sauce evenly between 2 hot sterilized widemouthed pint jars, pressing down firmly on the mushrooms to pack tightly.

4. Seal with new lids and metal rings. Process in a hot-water bath (page 8) for 15 minutes. Remove, cool, check seals, label, and store. Season for 2 weeks before using.

SALSAS AND RELISHES

*S*alsas have taken the place of the relishes of the 1950s and 1960s. As foods from Mexico and Central America spread throughout the United States, salsas came to nearly every community. Salsa, the Spanish word for sauce or gravy, is now considered a generic term for a finely chopped blend of brightly colored fruits and/or vegetables. The small bowl of tomatoes, garlic, chilies, and cilantro, which used to be associated only with Mexican restaurants, now has a much broader application. In the absence of creamed and butter-rich sauces served with meat and fish, the new salsas fill the need for something lighter and yet flavorful to go with a grilled or broiled entree. And they come from various cuisines: mango-based chutneys from India served with lamb, cold tomato salsa topping highly seasoned pork from the Yucatán, cucumber and dill sauce for poached salmon from Scandinavia.

BLACK BEAN AND CORN SALSA

It makes perfect sense to scoop a crisp tortilla chip into this delicious
vegetable mixture, but fill a cup-shaped radicchio leaf with a heaping
spoonful and you will have a sensationally colored salad. Being a lover
of soft tacos, I have often lunched on a corn tortilla rolled around
this salsa and sprinkled with a little Monterey Jack cheese. When
ready to serve the salsa, stir in some fresh cilantro for a "just made"
flavor.

Makes 4 pint jars

3 cups dried black beans, soaked
    overnight in water to cover
    (about 1 pound)

1 1/2 teaspoons salt

2 cloves garlic

4 cups corn kernels (6 to 7 ears
    of corn)

1 cup finely chopped red bell
    pepper

1 fresh jalapeño chili, seeds
    removed, finely chopped

1/2 cup finely chopped scallions,
    including part of the green

3 tablespoons red wine vinegar

1 tablespoon balsamic vinegar

3 tablespoons fresh lime juice

3 tablespoons olive oil

1 teaspoon sugar

1/4 teaspoon coarsely ground
    black pepper

1/2 teaspoon dried ground
    coriander

1 teaspoon dried oregano

1/2 cup coarsely chopped fresh
    cilantro

1. Drain the beans and put them into a large saucepan with 1 teaspoon salt and the garlic. Add water to cover by 1 inch and cook over medium heat until tender to the bite but still firm, about 1 hour. Drain. Discard the garlic.

2. Place the beans in a 12-inch nonreactive skillet with the corn, red pepper, jalapeño, scallions, and ½ cup of water. Simmer over low heat, uncovered, for 5 minutes. Stir in the vinegars, lime juice, olive oil, sugar, ½ teaspoon salt, pepper, coriander, oregano, and cilantro. Bring to a boil and cook 5 minutes more. Spoon into hot sterilized pint jars, leaving ½ inch head room.

3. Wipe the rims clean with a damp towel. Seal with new lids and metal rings. Process in a hot-water bath (page 8) for 15 minutes. Remove, cool, check seals, label, and store.

BLACK-EYED PEA SALSA

Black-eyed peas, really a kind of bean, can be made into a zingy salsa. The dried chilies, which vary in hotness, can be found in Latin American markets and specialty food shops. If only one variety is available, use that. This is a hearty salsa that can double as an hors d'oeuvre with fried tortilla chips or make a delicious filling for a tamale or soft corn tortilla. Before serving, sprinkle it with fresh cilantro. If you are going to use the salsa within two days, pour it into a bowl, cover, and store in the refrigerator. Sealing it in a jar means, among other things, that you can put together a gift basket including dried cornhusks, a recipe for tamales, Mexican oregano, masa harina, a can of mild green chilies, a bag of chips or fresh tortillas all tied up with some decorative Mexican crepe-paper flowers.

Makes 2 pint jars

3 cups dried black-eyed peas (about 1 pound)

1 1/2 teaspoons salt

1 dried pasilla chili

1 dried chili negro or Anaheim chili

1/4 cup homemade Dried Tomatoes in Olive Oil (page 122) or store-bought dried tomatoes packed in oil, diced

1 cup chopped fresh seeded tomatoes

2 teaspoons mild chili powder

1 tablespoon red wine vinegar

1/2 teaspoon ground cumin

1/4 teaspoon coarsely ground black pepper

1 tablespoon finely chopped cilantro, for garnish, if desired

1. Wash the peas and pick through for any stones. Cook, uncovered, in a medium saucepan over medium heat in 6 cups water and 1 teaspoon salt for 45 minutes until tender. Drain and reserve liquid.

2. Pull off the stems of the chilies and shake out the seeds. Soak the chilies in 2 cups boiling water until soft, about 30 minutes. Remove any seeds. Puree with 1 cup of the soaking liquid in a food processor.

3. Combine the peas, 1½ cups of the reserved cooking liquid, chili puree, dried tomatoes, fresh tomatoes, chili powder, vinegar, ½ teaspoon salt, cumin, and black pepper in a 2-quart bowl. Stir until well combined. Pour into a nonreactive saucepan and bring to a boil. Spoon into 2 hot sterilized widemouthed pint jars, filling to within ½ inch of the top.

4. Wipe the rims clean with a damp towel. Seal with new lids and metal rings. Process in a hot-water bath (page 8) for 15 minutes. Remove, cool, check seals, label, and store.

PAPAYA-MANGO SALSA

Fruit-based salsas are particularly well suited to grilled fish. This one was created by my son, Brad, a talented young chef in Santa Monica, California. This salsa is best on a meaty fish such as swordfish, mahimahi, shark, ahi, or bluefish.

Makes 2 pint jars

2 ripe but firm papayas, peeled, halved, and seeded (about 1 pound each)

2 large ripe mangoes, peeled (about 1 1/4 pounds each)

1 cup unsweetened pineapple juice

2 tablespoons fresh lime juice

1 tablespoon rice wine vinegar

2 tablespoons finely chopped Crystallized Gingerroot (page 129), rinsed

1/2 teaspoon salt

2 jalapeño chilies, preferably red, seeded, and minced

1 tablespoon finely chopped fresh mint leaves

1. Cut the papayas into 1/2-inch dice and place in a large nonreactive saucepan. Cut the peeled mangoes lengthwise into strips 1/2 inch wide against the pit. Cut crosswise to form 1/2-inch cubes. Scrape the knife along the pit to free the diced pulp. Add to the saucepan.

2. Stir in the pineapple juice, lime juice, vinegar, gingerroot, salt, jalapeños, and mint. Bring to a boil over medium heat and immediately pour into 2 hot sterilized jars to within 1/2 inch of the top.

3. Wipe the rims clean with a damp towel. Seal with new lids and metal rings. Process in a hot-water bath (page 8) for 15 minutes. Remove, cool, check seals, label, and store.

ITALIAN SALSA

Inspired by all those olives in Italian markets, I combined them with other Italian ingredients to make this salsa. It can be included in an antipasto platter, stirred into warm pasta, or spread on a grilled piece of country bread. It keeps well in the refrigerator for several weeks, but to keep it longer or to be able to give it away, put it up in canning jars.

Makes 3 pint jars

8 ounces Kalamata olives, pitted

8 ounces large green olives, pitted

1 red bell pepper, cut into 2-inch pieces

1/2 cup chopped Dried Tomatoes in Olive Oil, homemade (page 122) or store-bought

1 teaspoon dried oregano

2 tablespoons chopped flat-leaf parsley

3 cloves garlic, minced

2 tablespoons red wine vinegar

1 tablespoon balsamic vinegar

1/3 cup extra-virgin olive oil

1/4 teaspoon coarsely ground black pepper

1. Combine the olives, red pepper, and tomatoes in a food processor in 2 batches and pulse to a finely chopped texture. Do not puree.

2. Transfer to a medium nonreactive saucepan and stir in the oregano, parsley, garlic, vinegars, oil, and black pepper. Heat just until mixture comes to a boil and spoon into hot sterilized jars. Seal with new lids and metal rings. Wipe the rims clean with a damp towel.

3. Process in a hot-water bath (page 8) for 15 minutes. Remove, cool, check seals, label, and store.

ROASTED GREEN CHILI SALSA

Because this salsa is pureed instead of chunky, it makes a fine sauce for enchiladas or grilled chicken. I've even served it with corn fritters. If Anaheim chilies are not in your market, select another variety with a mild flavor.

Makes 2 pint jars

4 large green chilies, preferably
   Anaheims

2 small onions, finely chopped

4 tablespoons olive oil

6 cloves garlic, minced

2 large or 3 medium tomatoes,
   seeded and diced (about
   1 pound)

4 tablespoons tomato paste

1 teaspoon salt

1 1/2 teaspoons dried ground
   coriander

1/4 teaspoon crushed red pepper

1/2 teaspoon chili powder

1. Broil the chilies on a baking sheet 4 inches from the heat for 30 minutes, turning to blacken all sides. Remove, and when cool enough to handle, remove the stems and seeds.

2. Sauté the onions in olive oil in a large nonreactive saucepan over medium heat until soft. Add the garlic and cook, stirring, for 3 to 4 minutes more.

3. Puree the chilies and tomatoes in a food processor. Add the puree, the tomato paste, salt, coriander, red pepper, and chili powder to the onions. Cook for 20 minutes, stirring occasionally, until the mixture has thickened slightly. Ladle into 2 hot sterilized pint jars. Wipe the rims clean with a damp towel.

4. Seal with new lids and metal rings. Process in a hot-water bath (page 8) for 15 minutes. Remove, cool, check seals, label, and store.

ZUCCHINI AND ROASTED CORN SALSA

Bright fresh tastes and summer colors are present in this salsa; it looks like confetti. This is a very low calorie version that is still true to Mexican flavors. Serve it with homemade corn tortilla chips or make a summer salad by adding strips of grilled chicken and shredded lettuce.

Makes 2 pint jars

3 medium zucchini
  (1 1/4 pounds)

1 1/2 teaspoons salt

2 large ears of corn

4 tablespoons olive oil

2 jalapeño chilies, seeded and
  minced

2 medium tomatoes, seeded and
  finely chopped (about
  1 pound)

1 tablespoon fresh lime juice

2 cloves garlic, minced

1/4 teaspoon coarsely ground
  black pepper

1/4 cup finely chopped scallions,
  including part of the green

1. Preheat the oven to 400° F.

2. Cut off the ends of the zucchini and cut in half lengthwise. Slice 1/4 inch thick and then cut into 1/4-inch dice. Toss with 1 teaspoon salt and drain in a colander for 30 minutes. Rinse and pat dry.

3. Remove the husks from the corn and lightly coat with 2 teaspoons of olive oil. Place the corn on a baking sheet and roast for 30 to 40 minutes, or until the kernels are golden brown. Remove and cool to room temperature. Cut the kernels off the cobs, scraping to remove any additional corn liquid.

4. Combine the zucchini, corn, jalapeños, tomatoes, lime juice, garlic, pepper, scallions, and the remaining salt and olive oil in a large bowl. Pour into a nonreactive saucepan and bring just to a boil over medium heat. Immediately ladle into hot sterilized jars. Wipe the rims clean with a damp towel.

5. Seal with new lids and metal rings. Process in a hot-water bath (page 8) for 15 minutes. Remove, cool, check seals, label, and store.

WHITE CORN RELISH

As long as I can remember, my grandmother and my mother served their homemade corn relish with baked ham. It also goes well with pork roast, turkey, or fried chicken. This particular version came from my great-grandmother; the only changes I have made are the addition of a jalapeño chili and a squeeze of lime. Be sure to use white corn; it's much sweeter and more tender than the yellow. This relish can also be served as a salsa with tortilla chips. My daughter, Jennifer, claims it greatly improves a tuna salad.

Makes 5 pint jars

9 ears white corn (6 cups kernels)
1/2 medium head green cabbage
4 medium onions
3 green bell peppers
1 red bell pepper
1 jalapeño chili
2/3 cup sugar

4 teaspoons salt
1/4 cup prepared mustard, not Dijon
1/2 teaspoon celery seed
3/4 cup white vinegar
1 tablespoon fresh lime juice
1/4 teaspoon ground mace

1. Cut the corn from the cobs and scrape the cobs over a large bowl to remove any additional liquid.

2. Finely shred the cabbage, then finely chop it by hand or use the fine shredding blade of a food processor, then pulse it until chopped fine. Add to the bowl with the corn.

3. Finely chop the onions and green and red peppers. Remove the seeds from the jalapeño and mince. Add to the other vegetables in the bowl.

4. Mix together the vegetables, sugar, salt, mustard, celery seed, vinegar, lime juice, and mace in a large nonreactive skillet or Dutch oven. Bring to a boil and cook, stirring constantly, for 30 to 40 minutes. Spoon into hot sterilized jars. Wipe the rims clean with a damp towel.

5. Seal with new lids and metal rings. Process in a hot-water bath (page 8) for 15 minutes. Remove, cool, check seals, label, and store. Season for 2 weeks before using.

FENNEL AND SWEET ONION RELISH

Several types of milder onion are available now: the Spanish red, the white Maui, and the yellow Vidalia, among others. They can be made even sweeter by the presence of fennel. This relish is perfect on an open roast beef sandwich on rye or spread on toasted Italian bread and sprinkled with Parmesan.

Makes 2 pint jars

1 pound mild sweet onions, such as Maui, Vidalia, or Spanish red

2 teaspoons kosher or pickling salt

1 bulb fennel ($^{3}/_{4}$ pound)

1 cup white wine vinegar

3 tablespoons sugar

2 bay leaves

$^{1}/_{4}$ teaspoon coarsely ground pepper

1 tablespoon chopped flat-leaf parsley

1. Slice the onions very thin, toss with 1 teaspoon of the salt, and place in a colander to drain for 2 hours. Rinse well and drain.

2. Cut the fennel bulb in half through the stem end and thinly slice each half, including any feathery greens. Toss with the onions.

3. Heat the vinegar and 1 cup of water to a boil in a nonreactive saucepan. Add the sugar, bay leaves, pepper, and remaining salt. Boil for 5 minutes. Stir in the parsley and the onion mixture. Spoon into hot sterilized widemouthed pint jars, pouring in enough liquid to come within ½ inch of the top. Press down on the onions and fennel to submerge them completely under the pickling liquid. Wipe the rims clean with a damp towel.

4. Seal with new lids and metal rings. Process in a hot-water bath (page 8) for 15 minutes. Remove, cool, check seals, label, and store.

DRIED AND CANDIED: FRUITS, VEGETABLES, AND HERBS

y far the simplest method of preserving food is drying. There is no special equipment, no mixing, no jars, no extra shelf space required. Long, hot sunny days or low heat in an oven and a flat surface on which to spread the fruit are all that are necessary. Dried cranberries, blueberries, and cherries can replace raisins in many dessert recipes, adding intense new tastes. Dried vegetables such as high-moisture tomatoes and eggplant should be dried until they have shrunk to about one-third their original size and still remain pliable. Because my husband and I love freshly squeezed grapefruit juice, I decided to make use of all the discarded rinds. Candied citrus peels are that sweet/tart combination that tastes so refreshing. Equally delicious made from the thick-skinned winter navel orange or lemon, candied peels can be stored airtight for six months.

DRIED TOMATOES IN OLIVE OIL

For the last four years I have had the privilege and pleasure of working for chef Mark Peel of Campanile restaurant. This is his recipe, and one that I could not improve on. When the price of a jar of sundried tomatoes packed in olive oil exceeds the cost of the entree you're serving, you feel very smug to know you made them yourself. Choose Italian plum or Roma tomatoes, which are meatier and have less liquid than regular tomatoes. The tomatoes will keep in the refrigerator for several weeks. Don't be alarmed if the oil solidifies; it will liquefy again when brought to room temperature.

Makes 2 pint jars

6 pounds Italian plum or Roma
   tomatoes (about 40)

2 teaspoons kosher salt

1/2 teaspoon coarsely ground
   black pepper

1/2 cup whole basil leaves

1/4 cup capers

2 cups extra-virgin olive oil

1. Slice the tomatoes in half through the stem end and lay, skin side down, on 2 rimmed baking sheets, wedging in as tightly as possible. Sprinkle lightly with salt and pepper and place on a rack in the upper third of the oven. Turn the oven to the lowest possible setting and leave undisturbed for 24 hours. Check to see if the tomatoes have shrunk to a third of their original size and all the moisture has

evaporated from the center. If they still feel spongy, continue drying for 8 to 10 hours more, or until they are flat and shriveled but not crisp. Remove from the oven and cool to room temperature.

2. Tightly layer the tomatoes, basil leaves, and capers in hot sterilized jars. Pour in the olive oil, filling to within $\frac{1}{2}$ inch of the top. Wipe rims clean with a damp towel. Seal with new lids and metal rings.

3. Process in a hot-water bath (page 8) for 15 minutes. Remove, cool, check seals, label, and store.

OVEN-DRIED HERBED EGGPLANT SLICES

I love eggplant. And growing up, I was the only one in my family who did. Fortunately, my husband and children like eggplant almost as much as I do, so there's usually always one (or two) in the refrigerator. Some days when I feel industrious and small Japanese eggplants are in all the farmers' markets and I don't really want the mess of real canning, I dry and freeze some. I pack them in family-size proportions and take them directly from the freezer to place on pizza shells, add to a Mediterranean salad, or stir into a hearty marinara sauce.

Makes about 50 slices

3 pounds Japanese eggplant, sliced ½ inch thick

½ teaspoon kosher salt

¼ teaspoon coarsely ground black pepper

2 tablespoons finely chopped fresh basil leaves

1 tablespoon finely chopped fresh marjoram

1 tablespoon finely chopped fresh thyme

⅓ cup olive oil

1. Preheat the oven to its lowest setting.

2. Spread the eggplant slices in a single layer on 2 oiled baking sheets. Stir together the salt, pepper, basil, marjoram, thyme, and oil in a small bowl. Using a pastry brush, lightly coat both sides of the eggplant with the herb mixture.

3. Place the baking sheets in the center of the oven and leave undisturbed for 24 hours. Slices will appear wrinkled and slightly crisp around the edges but soft in the center.

4. Remove from the oven and cool completely to room temperature. Pack in freezer bags, expelling as much air as possible, and freeze.

DRIED CRANBERRIES OR BLUEBERRIES

Dried fruit other than raisins is starting to appear in muffins, scones, and granola: dried cranberries, blueberries, and sour cherries. When the moisture of the fruit is removed, the flavor is intensified. These dried berries are tart; commercially dried berries are made with added corn syrup. Since each berry is a slightly different size, check about every hour and remove the ones that are ready. They will be wrinkled and deflated-looking and will no longer stain the hands when gently squeezed; they should not be so dry that they feel crisp or weightless.

Makes ¾ cup dried berries

12-ounce bag (2½ cups)
  cranberries or 2 cups (1 pint)
  blueberries

1. Preheat the oven to 200° F.

2. Wash the berries and remove any stems. Spread out in a single layer on a rimmed baking sheet and place in the center of the oven. After about 4 hours, check the berries every hour and shake the pan. After about 6 hours, some berries should be ready. Shrunken to about half their original size, they will have darkened and shriveled but still feel soft. Remove them to a plate to cool. Continue checking and removing the dried ones until all are done. This could take as long as 10 hours.

3. Store the dried berries in the refrigerator or freezer in a freezer bag. They will keep 8 weeks.

CANDIED GRAPEFRUIT PEEL

Employing the ying and yang of taste—sweet and sour—candied grapefruit peel is a versatile condiment. It will keep, covered, in the refrigerator for a year if left in its own syrup. It is a splendid replacement for the candied fruits in Christmas fruitcakes and a tingly addition to panforte. Use it where candied gingerroot might be used. Rolled in superfine sugar and airdried, the candied peel becomes a frosted translucent sweet, perfect with afternoon tea. Half-dipped in bittersweet chocolate, the peel is a most complex and sophisticated companion to espresso. This recipe works just as well with oranges.

Makes 1 quart

4 medium thin-skinned
  grapefruits
3 cups sugar

1. Cut a thin slice off each end of each grapefruit. With a sharp knife, make 4 vertical cuts through the peel to score it. Pull off the peel. Save the fruit for another use. Cut the peel into ¼-inch strips. Depending on the size of the grapefruits, the strips should be about 3 to 3½ inches long.

2. Stir the sugar into 3 cups of water in a 10-inch skillet or heavy shallow pan over medium heat. When the sugar is completely dissolved, add the grapefruit peel. Continue cooking, uncovered, until the peel is translucent and the syrup begins to foam, about 30

minutes. Do not cook until all the syrup has evaporated. Remove from the heat and cool to room temperature.

3. Pour into a jar or covered bowl, making sure all peel is submerged, and store in the refrigerator.

Sugar Dipped Candied Grapefruit Peel Select the straightest pieces of candied peel and lay out on a plate. Line a baking sheet with wax paper. Sprinkle 1 cup of superfine sugar into a shallow bowl. Drain excess syrup from each strip and then roll it through the sugar, coating all surfaces. Place on the prepared baking sheet and allow to dry at room temperature overnight. Store in an airtight tin for 1 month before using.

Chocolate Dipped Candied Grapefruit Peel Melt 8 ounces of fine imported bittersweet chocolate in the top of a double boiler over barely simmering water. Holding one end of a sugared (directions above) strip of grapefruit peel, dip and place on wax paper to harden. To completely coat with chocolate, hold the peel with a fork to dip into the chocolate and allow to drain briefly before laying on the wax paper. Store in an airtight tin.

Candied Orange Peel Substitute 8 large navel (thick-skinned) oranges for the grapefruit.

CRYSTALLIZED GINGERROOT

When you make any preserved gingerroot recipe, it is important to start with the very young or "yellow" gingerroot that is available in Chinese markets (and some supermarkets) in January and February and again in July and August. This gingerroot is very tender and moist, not so fibrous, with a thin pale skin tinged with pink. Crystallized gingerroot can be eaten as is or chopped and stirred into ice cream or added to a cookie or scone dough. It will keep indefinitely in a sealed container. This is an adaptation of a recipe by Bruce Cost from his book, *Ginger East to West*.

Makes 1 1/2 pounds

1 1/2 pounds young gingerroot
1 3/4 cups sugar
1 tablespoon fresh lemon juice
dash salt
additional sugar for coating,
  if desired

1. Cover the gingerroot, unpeeled, with cold water and soak overnight.

2. Drain, cover with fresh water, and bring to a boil. Reduce the heat and simmer for 10 minutes. Drain and cool. Peel the gingerroot and cut into 1/8-inch "coins." Cover with water and simmer for 10 minutes. Drain and repeat, then drain again.   *(continued)*

3. Place the sugar, lemon juice, and salt in a medium saucepan with 2½ cups water and bring to a boil. Reduce the heat and simmer until the sugar is dissolved. Add the gingerroot pieces, bring to a boil again, reduce the heat, and simmer for 5 minutes. Turn off the heat and allow the gingerroot to stand in the syrup for at least 1 hour.

4. Return to the heat and simmer, stirring occasionally, for at least 30 minutes, or until almost all of the liquid is absorbed. Begin stirring constantly at this point. When almost all the syrup has been absorbed and the gingerroot pieces are nearly dry, remove the pan from the heat and continue stirring for 5 minutes more.

5. Remove the pieces with small tongs or chopsticks to sheets of wax paper to cool and harden. The gingerroot can also be rolled in sugar when cool enough to handle. Store in an airtight container.

PRESERVING HERBS

Being a passionate gardener blessed with California sunshine, I try to grow whatever I need for my kitchen. But no matter where you live, herbs can adapt nicely to a windowsill or small plot near the back door. The pleasure is doubled when you dry a winter's supply of herbs that are frost sensitive or are grown as annuals. The intense flavors of herbs come from the oils released when they are gently crushed or cooked. Not all herbs contain a high percentage of oil and therefore are better used only in a fresh state, but the more pungent ones—rosemary, thyme, marjoram, sage, oregano, and tarragon—will retain much of their true essence after drying. Other herbs such as basil, mint, chives, and parsley are better frozen, or, in the case of basil, preserved in olive oil and refrigerated.

Even though they become limp and lose their color, herbs can be frozen in airtight plastic storage bags with very little loss of fresh flavor, but because they do turn black they are not suitable for garnishes or in salads. Wash, dry thoroughly, pack into bags without crushing, and freeze. Parsley, chives, or mint can be finely chopped and packed in a plastic container and scooped out by tablespoons as needed, and there's no need to thaw them before using.

Pestos, made from pureeing herbs with a binder of oil and nuts, are another way to preserve the intensity of an herbal flavor you enjoy. Pestos keep for several weeks in the refrigerator if covered with a thin film of olive oil. In a blender puree 2 cups of basil, cilantro, mint, dill, parsley, or oregano. Add garlic if you wish, ¼ cup of walnuts, pine nuts (pignolis), or almonds, and grind to a paste. With the blender running, pour in ½ cup olive oil until the mixture is smooth. Season with salt. A tablespoon at a time may be stirred into warm pasta, salad dressings, spread on fish fillets to be grilled.

You can also experiment with a combination of herbs. Using the proportions of Herbs de Provence, you can make a pesto or finely chop these herbs and add to softened cream cheese. Equal portions of marjoram, thyme, and summer savory, and half as much rosemary, sage, and parsley will combine into an aromatic blend of "flavors Provençal" that can be preserved in olive oil, a container in the freezer, in cheese, or in vinegar.

Gather herbs that are to be dried early in the day but after the dew has evaporated. Exposure to the sun will diminish the herbs' essential oils. Pick them just before they bloom, when they are at their aromatic peak. Rinse gently, shake dry, and discard any yellowed or blemished leaves. Tie small bunches together at the stem end and hang upside down in a cool, dimly lit, well-ventilated room. Several days should be enough unless the weather is excessively humid. For longer storage, place a small paper bag over the herb, tying at the stem end. This will protect the leaves from dust and catch any that may fall off. After the leaves are dry but not brown, strip them from the stems and crumble. They should feel as crisp as fresh cornflakes and still have their green color. The drying process may be completed in a warm oven with the door open for a couple of hours if you live in a particularly humid climate.

Store dried herbs in tightly lidded glass jars, preferably away from light. Discard any dried herbs you have had in your pantry for more than a year. Flavor and color will be at a minimum.

If you cultivate your own herbs, putting together a small bouquet for a sick friend can be a way of preserving the herbs and the friendship. The clean, woodsy smell of freshly picked herbs contributes to an aura of health and healing and is often more pleasing than sweet flowers. Snip sprigs of gray santolina, scented geranium, lamb's ears, flowering English thyme, English or French lavender, rosemary, and artemisia. Tie loosely together with a narrow satin ribbon and place in an old preserves jar or small vase. When the herbs begin to fade, tell your friend, simply pour out the water and hang the bouquet upside down for a few days. Then reuse it as a dried arrangement.

Branches of rosemary can be cut from a prolific bush to form small wreaths using floral wire as a base. Rosemary, the herb of remembrance, will bend easily into a heart- or circle-shaped wreath. Left unadorned or combined with other fresh herbs and flowers, which will dry into shape, a rosemary circlet will provide culinary inspiration and visual pleasure. Thyme and marjoram, although much more delicate, also make very charming and fragrant small wreaths for the kitchen.

HERBAL VINEGARS

*H*erbal vinegars are another way to prolong the life of summer herbs. They are beautiful, add sparkle to a variety of dishes, and are out-of-season reminders of tastes and smells from the garden. They can be used to deglaze a pan, marinate vegetables and chicken, splash over poached salmon, or drizzle over tomatoes and mozzarella. Salads dressed with herbal vinegars echo the fresh tastes that were alive not long ago in your garden. A dash of herbal vinegar in the poaching water for an egg not only keeps the white from spreading but gives the egg a savory tinge. When making an herbal vinegar, always start with a good vinegar—white or red wine, champagne, rice, or cider—and the freshest herbs. Distilled white vinegar is too harsh and balsamic vinegar already has a distinct sweetness. If you are growing your own herbs, pick them early in the day, wash and gently pat or air dry. Herbs that are about to flower are at their peak of taste. Braise the herbs, heat the vinegar until hot but not boiling, and pour it over the herbs. Cover the jar with plastic wrap to eliminate the risk of corrosion of a metal lid. Place the jar in a cool dark place for several weeks, swirling occasionally. Taste the vinegar and if you feel it is right, strain it into a clean, sterilized bottle. Vinegars last indefinitely.

I have found that Perrier bottles, both large and small, fitted with ordinary wine corks, either used and cleaned or purchased at the hardware store, make perfect containers for home-bottled vinegars to keep or give as gifts. The green glass cuts down on deterioration from light. Another recyclable container is the sixteen-ounce Grolsch beer bottle with a ceramic swing-away top. Beautiful reproductions of antique bottles can be found at cookware stores, but saving used bottles is less expensive. Wash the bottles and sterilize them by pouring boiling water into them. Allow to stand for ten minutes, then turn the bottles upside down to dry. Insert fresh sprigs of herbs when filling the bottles and attach attractive labels. As you use the flavored vinegar, you can replace it with some of the base vinegar. It will not be as strong, but it will continue to take on the flavor.

The recipes in this chapter serve only as a starting point for your imagination. There is no chemistry involved here except the rules of using clean bottles and washed herbs. How strong you wish your vinegars to be flavored is a matter of preference. Most should be tasted after four weeks. At that time you can strain the vinegar into a clean bottle or allow it to season a little longer.

OPAL BASIL VINEGAR

Opal basil is a broad-leaf variety with the most amazing color. Although its flavor is less pungent than the smaller sweet basil, the dark red purple leaves are a striking accent in salad, pasta, or vinegar. Just a few sprigs will turn a bottle of vinegar garnet red. If you can't find enough of the basil for this recipe, cut the proportions in half. It's a must!

Makes 1 quart

4 cups rice wine vinegar
2 cups (lightly packed) opal
  basil leaves, including
  blossoms but not woody stems,
  washed and patted dry

1. Heat the vinegar in a nonreactive saucepan but do not boil.

2. Put the basil leaves in a widemouthed quart (or larger) jar and bruise with a wooden spoon. Pour in the vinegar and cool to room temperature. Cover with plastic wrap and secure with string or a rubber band. Leave in a cool, dimly lit place for 4 weeks or longer, occasionally swirling the contents.

3. When ready to use, strain through 2 layers of damp cheesecloth into a clean sterilized bottle. Insert a fresh sprig of basil and cap or cork.

NASTURTIUM AND PEPPER VINEGAR

Nasturtium flowers and leaves have a natural peppery bite. Combining them with peppercorns and dried chili peppers emphasizes this characteristic and makes an assertive vinegar. I like this taste in a vinaigrette for marinating seafood or chicken, on tomatoes, or in salsa. The nasturtium blossoms turn the vinegar a beautiful shade of crimson. Rice wine vinegar tempers the peppers' fire.

Makes 1 quart

4 cups nasturtium blossoms, mixed colors, washed and dried

3 tablespoons whole peppercorns

8 dried red chilies

4 cups rice wine vinegar

1. Place the nasturtiums in a widemouthed quart (or larger) jar, packing down and lightly bruising with a wooden spoon. Spread the peppercorns on a cutting board and crush with the bottom of a heavy pan. Add the peppercorns and dried chilies to the nasturtiums.

2. Heat the vinegar in a medium saucepan but do not boil. Pour into the jar, cover with plastic wrap, and secure with string or a rubber band. Leave in a cool, dimly lit place for 4 weeks, occasionally swirling the contents.

3. Reheat the vinegar with the other ingredients. Pour through a fine-mesh strainer or 2 layers of damp cheesecloth into clean, sterilized jars. Place several fresh nasturtiums in each jar and cap or cork.

ORANGE–THYME VINEGAR

I felt the sweet character of orange and the mellow taste of lemon thyme would combine well with champagne vinegar, and I was right. The whole sprigs of thyme and thick shards of orange peel make the vinegar handsome to look at too. Because of the subtle nature of the two flavors, this vinegar requires at least two months to develop fully.

Makes 1 quart

4 cups champagne vinegar

20 strips orange peel, trimmed of white pith, 3 inches × ¹/₂ inch

1 cup (well-packed) sprigs fresh lemon thyme or regular thyme

10 whole cloves

1 bay leaf

2 strips fresh orange rind for final bottling

3 sprigs fresh lemon or regular thyme for final bottling

1. Heat the vinegar with the orange peel in a nonreactive saucepan until very hot but not boiling. Place the thyme, cloves, and bay leaf in a clean jar and gently bruise with a wooden spoon. Pour in the vinegar and peel and stir to combine. Cool to room temperature. Cover tightly with plastic wrap and secure with string or a rubber band. Store in a cool dark place for at least 2 months. Occasionally swirl contents around in jar.

2. To transfer to a decorative bottle, strain the vinegar into a clean, sterilized bottle and insert the fresh strips of orange rind and fresh sprigs of thyme. Cork or cap the bottle tightly.

RASPBERRY-ROSE GERANIUM VINEGAR

After sampling a salad strewn with nasturtiums, pansies, and thyme blossoms, I decided to try to make a flavored vinegar that would take advantage of the trend of eating flowers. I started imagining red raspberries together with red roses and then I thought of the rose geranium, whose leaf smells like the most fragrant of roses. If you can't find rose geranium leaves, substitute an equal amount of pesticide-free very fragrant red rose petals.

Makes 1 quart

4 cups red wine vinegar
1 cup rose geranium leaves, washed and patted dry
2 cups raspberries

$^1/_4$ cup raspberries for final bottling
1 or 2 fresh geranium leaves for final bottling

1. Heat the vinegar and geranium leaves in a nonreactive saucepan until hot but not boiling. Place the raspberries in a widemouthed quart (or larger) jar and crush lightly with a wooden spoon. Pour in the hot vinegar and geranium leaves. Cover the jar with plastic wrap and secure with string or a rubber band. Season for at least 2 weeks in a cool, dimly lit place, swirling contents occasionally.

2. Strain the vinegar through a sieve lined with 2 layers of dampened cheesecloth into a sterilized bottle. Drop in the fresh raspberries and a fresh geranium leaf. Cap or cork the bottle.

MINT AND ROSEMARY VINEGAR

When I put these herbs together in a red wine vinegar, I must have been visualizing a lamb marinade. But then it occurred to me that this vinegar can be used to make a very English mint sauce or for deglazing the pan after sautéing lamb chops. And, of course, it can be used in a vinaigrette for a salad of mixed baby lettuces.

Makes 1 quart

4 cups red wine vinegar

2 teaspoons sugar

2 cups (loosely packed) fresh mint leaves

1 cup fresh rosemary needles

1 sprig fresh rosemary for final bottling

1 sprig fresh mint for final bottling

1. Heat together the vinegar and sugar in a medium saucepan just to a boil. Place the mint and rosemary in a clean jar and lightly bruise with a wooden spoon. Pour in the hot vinegar and let cool. Cover with plastic wrap fastened with string or a rubber band. Store in a cool, dimly lit place for at least 4 weeks, swirling the contents of the jar occasionally.

2. Strain through a fine-mesh strainer or dampened cheesecloth into a sterilized decorative bottle. Insert a fresh sprig of rosemary and mint.

INDEX

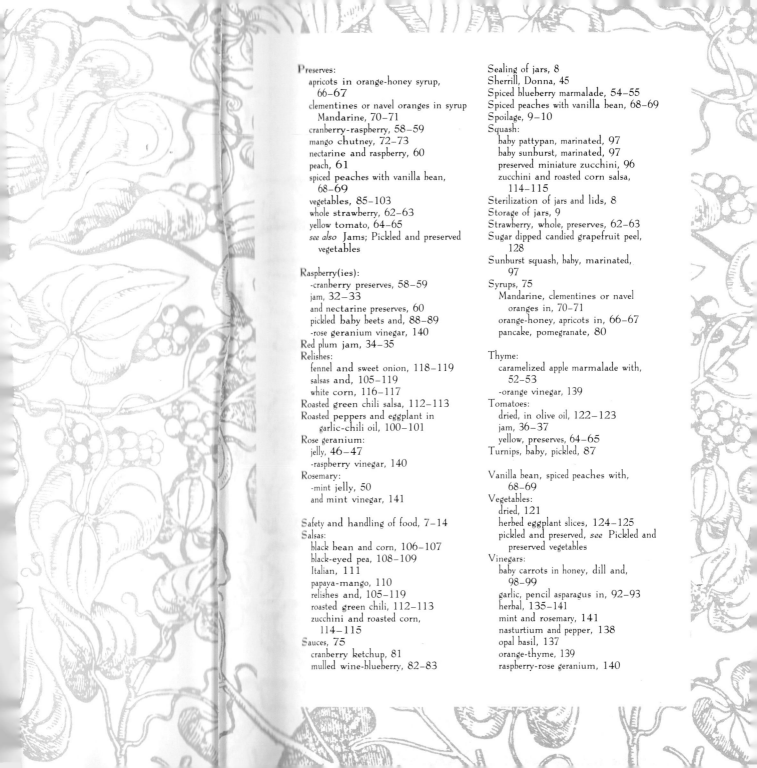